ZEPPELIN
VS
BRITISH HOME DEFENCE

1915–18

JON GUTTMAN

OSPREY

Bloomsbury Publishing Plc

PO Box 883, Oxford, OX1 9PL, UK

1385 Broadway, 5th Floor, New York, NY 10018, USA

E-mail: info@ospreypublishing.com

www.ospreypublishing.com

OSPREY is a trademark of Osprey Publishing Ltd

First published in Great Britain in 2018

© Osprey Publishing Ltd, 2018

A catalogue record for this book is available from the British Library.

ISBN: PB: 978 1 4728 2033 4; eBook 978 1 4728 2035 8; ePDF 978 1 4728 2034 1; XML 978 1 4728 2194 2

18 19 20 21 22 10 9 8 7 6 5 4 3 2 1

Edited by Tony Holmes
Cover artwork, three-views, cockpits, battlescene, Engaging the Enemy and armament scrap views by Jim Laurier
Maps and formation diagrams by Bounford Ltd
Index by Zoe Ross
Typeset by PDQ Digital Media Solutions, Bungay, UK
Printed in China through World Print Ltd

Osprey Publishing supports the Woodland Trust, the UK's leading woodland conservation charity. Between 2014 and 2018 our donations are being spent on their Centenary Woods project in the UK.

To find out more about our authors and books visit **www.ospreypublishing. com**. Here you will find extracts, author interviews, details of forthcoming events and the option to sign up for our newsletter.

Zeppelin cover art

On 23 September 1916, 12 Zeppelin airships of the *Kaiserliche Marine* (Imperial German Navy) attacked England, with eight bombing the Midlands and four new 'Super Zeppelins' making for London. *L.32* was caught in searchlights over Tilbury, attracting the attention of 2Lt Frederick Sowrey of No. 39 (Home Defence) Sqn in BE 2c 4112. Pursuing the airship as it rose and tried to manoeuvre away from the searchlights, Sowrey sprayed two drums of Lewis machine-gun fire along its underside without effect, which he found 'rather disheartening'. With his third magazine, however, he emulated what squadronmate 2Lt William Leefe Robinson had done to bring down Schütte-Lanz airship *SL.11* 21 days earlier and concentrated his fire on one area. He reported seeing a deep rosy glow within the Zeppelin that made it look like a 'huge Chinese lantern', followed by fiery explosions and a blazing descent that narrowly missed his aeroplane as its remains crashed at Great Burstead in Essex, killing Oblt-z-S Werner Petersen and his 21 crewmen.

BE 2c artwork

L.33, under Kptltn der R Aloys Böcker, was one of four new 'Super Zeppelins' that bombed London on the night of 23 September 1916. Targeting an oil depot, *L.33* was caught in searchlights and bracketed by anti-aircraft shells, which destroyed its No. 14 fuel cell and ruptured several others. As *L.33* struggled homeward, the airship dropped its last four bombs on No. 39 (Home Defence) Sqn's aerodrome at Hainault Farm in Essex. At 1213 hrs it was attacked over Chelmsford by BE 2c 4544 of No. 39 (Home Defence) Sqn, flown by 2Lt Albert de Bathe Brandon. Initially, the pilot's Lewis machine gun had jerked out of its mounting when he opened fire. However, Brandon quickly seated it once again, passed under the airship from the bow and then turned back into it and opened fired from behind and below. 'The Brock ammunition seemed to be bursting all along it but the Zepp did not catch fire', he later reported. 'I was using Brock, Pomeroy and Sparklet. I turned again and put on a fresh drum, before coming back up from behind and firing again. The gun jammed after nine rounds'. The only German to notice Brandon's attack was the upper rear gunner, who trained his weapon on the BE 2c but dared not fire for fear of igniting the hydrogen whose hissing escape he sensed all around him. At 1233 hrs, Brandon lost sight of his quarry against 'a large bank of grey cloud all around the horizon', but the damage was done. *L.33* came down near New Hall farm in Essex, where Böcker set it afire and marched his 20 men toward Colchester to surrender.

Acknowledgments

Thanks to Carl Bobrow, Christophe Cony, Philip Jarrett, Colin Owers, Steve Suddaby and Greg VanWyngarden for their assistance in preparing this volume.

Equivalent ranks and abbreviations

German rank	abbreviation	British rank	abbreviation
Kaiserliche Marine			
Fregattenkapitän	Frgkpt	Captain	Capt
Korvettenkapitän	Kvtkpt	Commander	Cdr
Kapitänleutnant	Kptltn	Lieutenant Commander	Lt Cdr
Oberleutnant-zur-See	Oblt-z-S	Lieutenant	Lt
Deutsche Luftstreitkräfte			
Oberst		Colonel	Col
Oberstleutnant	Obstltn	Lieutenant Colonel	Lt Col
Major	Maj	Major	Maj
Hauptmann	Hptm	Captain	Capt
Oberleutnant	Oblt	Lieutenant	Lt

CONTENTS

INTRODUCTION

Britain's first inkling that the English Channel was no longer the watery barrier it had been in ages past came on 17 January 1785, when Jean-Pierre Blanchard and John Jeffries flew across it in a hydrogen balloon. In that same year, Lt Jean Baptiste Meusnier of the French Corps of Engineers conceptualized an elliptical gasbag using hand-cranked propellers for both propulsion and steering, although he could not raise the funds to realize it. That would have to wait until 9 August 1884, when French Capitaines Charles Renard and Arthur Krebs unveiled the first successful airship, a streamlined hydrogen envelope with an electric motor running a four-bladed airscrew that propelled it at up to 15mph for 23 minutes. In the early 1900s, Alberto Santos-Dumont perfected a steerable airship using a gasoline engine, which he flew all around Paris.

On 2 July 1900, Germany grandly outdid them all as *Luftschiff Zeppelin LZ.1*, a rigid hydrogen airship incorporating an aluminium-zinc alloy framework 420ft long and 38ft in diameter, and powered by two 14hp Daimler engines, rose above Lake Constance, culminating ten years of obsessed experimentation by its creator, Ferdinand *Graf* von Zeppelin. His achievement would be emulated in 1905 by August von Parseval's keeled semi-rigid airship and in 1909 by *SL.1*, the first of a series of rigid airships using a wire-braced wooden framework devised by the Schütte-Lanz *Luftschiffsbau*.

At last freed of its tether, the airship could carry passengers and cargo anywhere within the range of its fuel supply. Whether its inventors approved or not, the airship's military application swiftly followed, as the balloon's ability to spy on enemy forces, utilized since 1794, could now be self-projected deep into his territory.

After 1903, that potential would be challenged by the emergence of another innovation – the heavier-than-air craft. Both airship and aeroplane would undergo

a spurt of rapid development in World War I, largely because it pitted them against each other. The prospect of aerial attack had been anticipated as early as 1899, when The Hague Declaration prohibited future combatants from 'launching projectiles from balloons or other kinds of aerial vessels'. Although 44 nations signed it then, only 27 of them signed the renewal in 1907, one of the abstainers being Germany.

In 1908, Britain began planning for aerial attack – a prospect made even more plausible on 25 July 1909, when Louis Blériot flew his monoplane across the Channel. By 1910, the British had added 3in and 4in artillery and 1-pounder pom-pom guns, capable of being directed skyward from makeshift high-angle platforms or from trucks, to its defences.

On 4 August 1914, the *Deutsches Heer* (Imperial German Army) marched into Belgium, and Britain, sworn by treaty to safeguard Belgian neutrality, declared war. In the face of continuing Belgian resistance, the Germans committed bloody depredations that fed an Allied propaganda campaign representing them as scourges of civilization – 'Huns', as the British called them. Those 'atrocities' included a bombing raid on the fortress town of Liège by army Zeppelin *Z.VI* on 6 August, killing nine civilians, and night attacks on Antwerp on 25 August and 2 September.

Zeppelin airship *LZ.1* makes its first ascent over Lake Constance on 2 July 1900. (Library of Congress)

As early as August 1914, Konteradmiral Paul Behncke, deputy chief of the German naval staff, proposed bombing Britain. He was supported by Grossadmiral Alfred von Tirpitz, who wrote, 'The measure of success will lie not only in the injury which will be caused to the enemy but also by the significant effect it will have in diminishing the enemy's determination to prosecute the war'. Kaiser Wilhelm II balked on approving the plan until 7 January 1915, and even then forbade attacks on London, lest they endanger his relatives in the Royal Family.

On the night of 19 January 1915, naval Zeppelins *L.6*, *L.3* and *L.4* left Fuhlsbüttel and Nordholz to cross the North Sea. *L.6* had to turn back, but *L.3* dropped nine high-explosive bombs on Great Yarmouth in Norfolk, while *L.4*'s incendiaries fell on King's Lynn and other Norfolk villages. The first airship raid on English soil caused two fatalities and 13 injuries, but minimal damage – and none to a military target. Nevertheless, four months before Italy entered the war, and long before its General Giulio Douhet publicly aired his theories on how the aerial bombing of enemy industries, resources and civilians could win wars, Germany set the precedent for a succession of raids on British cities, including the capital, London.

Although the material damage the Zeppelins did – and usually would do in future – was modest, the very arbitrary nature of the civilian casualties their bombs

LZ.5, which was adopted by the *Deutsches Heer* as *Z.II*, shown at Limburg in October 1910. (Greg VanWyngarden)

inflicted raised public outcries for the government to 'do something'. That in turn spurred the British to develop an air defence system that would ultimately incorporate searchlights, anti-aircraft artillery (AAA) and specially modified aeroplanes. It also compelled both the British Army and Royal Navy to divert at least some of their aerial assets from the Western Front to Home Defence. In that respect, the 'Zeppelin menace' constituted the first terror campaign to be waged from the air. Moreover, between the morale factor, the occasional damage done and the resources diverted to countering them, the Zeppelins can also lay claim to being history's first strategic bombers.

The irony to that distinction lies in the fact that giant airships swiftly proved to be grossly inefficient, hazardous and vulnerable vehicles for the task. By the end of 1916, British Home Defence had developed to a point whereby the terror went both ways, for while Britons wondered whether the next bomb falling in the night might have their names on it, Zeppelin crews crossed the Channel with a nagging qualm as to whether this latest sortie would be their last.

All in all, it was a unique air war, but one from which lessons would be learned that would be reapplied to bombing campaigns in the future – the sort that would pit aeroplane against aeroplane.

The *Deutsches Heer* crew of *Z.IX* (*LZ.25*), which reconnoitered and bombed its way over Belgium and northern France – including dropping nine bombs on Antwerp on 25 August 1914, killing 26 people and damaging the royal palace. Retribution came swiftly on 8 October, when Flt Lt Reginald Marix in a Sopwith Tabloid bombed and destroyed the airship in its shed at Düsseldorf. (Greg VanWyngarden)

CHRONOLOGY

1900
2 July   Ferdinand *Graf* von Zeppelin's first giant rigid airship achieves successful flight over Lake Constance.

1911
1 October   The first wooden-framed Schütte-Lanz airship, *SL.1*, flies at Rheinau, near Mannheim.

1914
6 August   Zeppelin *Z.VI* bombs Liège, killing nine civilians but causing no military damage.

25 August   Zeppelin airships bomb Antwerp.

5 September   First Lord of the Admiralty Winston Churchill outlines his Home Defence plan, with the Royal Navy responsible for defending London.

1 October   Blackout instructions go into effect in Britain

10 October   *Z.IX* bombed in its shed at Düsseldorf by Royal Naval Air Service (RNAS) pilot Flt Lt R. L. G. Marix in Sopwith Tabloid 168.

1915
19/20 January   First Zeppelin raid on British soil as *L.3* bombs Great Yarmouth, Norfolk.

Before finding its niche as a trainer, the Avro 504 saw combat use in 1914 as a reconnaissance aeroplane and as one of the bombers the RNAS used to strike at airship sheds. It later saw service in Home Defence squadrons, as exemplified by this 504K with Holt flares fitted under the wings and a Lewis machine gun mounted above the centre section of the upper wing. (Greg VanWyngarden)

5 May	Kaiser Wilhelm II extends airship targets to 'east of the Tower of London'.
31 May	*LZ.38*, commanded by Hptm Erich Linnartz, drops the first bombs on London, killing seven civilians, injuring 35 and causing £18,000 worth of damage.
6/7 June	*LZ.37* destroyed over Ghent by Flt Sub-Lt R. A. J. Warneford, who subsequently receives the Victoria Cross. *LZ.38* destroyed in its shed in Brussels-Evère by two Henry Farmans of A Squadron, 1 Wing, RNAS.
20 July	The Kaiser approves unrestricted bombing of London.
8/9 September	*L.13*, bombing from Bloomsbury to Liverpool Street Station, causes £534,387 worth of damage – the

most of all the airship raids on London.

12/14 October	*L.13*, *L.14* and *L.15*, dropping bombs from Covent Garden to Aldgate and on Woolwich and East Croyden, inflict the highest casualties of any airship raid, killing 71 and injuring 128.

1916

10 February	Responsibility for London's aerial defence passes from the Royal Navy to the Army.
15 May	The Royal Flying Corps (RFC) places its first large-scale order for Brock explosive ammunition.
2/3 September	2Lt William Leefe Robinson shoots down Schütte-Lanz *SL.11* over Cuffley, Hertfordshire, the airship being the first destroyed

LZ.7 Deutschland made considerable advances in the Zeppelin's design when it first flew on 19 June 1910, but its career with DELAG was short-lived, the airship being wrecked by a thunderstorm over the Teutoburg Forest on 28 June. (Library of Congress)

	over British soil. He receives the Victoria Cross for his exploit.
23/24 September	*L.33* forced to land by (AAA) fire and air attack in Essex. 2Lt Frederick Sowrey, in BE 2c 4112, destroys *L.32* near Great Burstead, Essex.
1/2 October	*L.31* destroyed by 2Lt W. J. Tempest in BE 2c 4577 near Potters Bar, Hertfordshire.
26/27 November	*L.34* shot down in flames by 2Lt I. V. Pyott in BE 2c 2738 off West Hartlepool, County Durham.
27/28 November	*L.21* lost at sea ten miles east of Lowestoft, Norfolk, after attack by Flt Lt E. Cadbury in BE 2c 8625 from Great Yarmouth.

1917

8 March	Ferdinand *Graf* von Zeppelin passes away, aged 78.
10 March	*L.42*, first of the 'Height Climber' Zeppelins, makes its maiden test flight, reaching an altitude of 19,700ft.
4 May	*L.22* is destroyed near Terschelling, one of the Dutch West Frisian islands, by Flt Cdr Robert Leckie and John Galpin in RNAS H-12B flying boat 8666.
13 June	First Gotha bomber raid on London.
13/14 June	*L.43* destroyed off Vrieland, on the Dutch coast, by B. D. Hobbes and R. F. L. Dickey in H-12 8677.
16/17 June	*L.48* is shot down near Theburton, Suffolk, by an FE 2b, a DH 2 and a BE 12.
27 August	*L.23* is shot down in flames by Flt

	Sub-Lt B. A. Smart in Sopwith Pup N6430 launched from the light cruiser HMS *Yarmouth*.
19/20 October	'Silent Raid' features the last airship attack on London as *L.45* bombs Hendon, Cricklewood, Piccadilly, Camberwell and Hither Green, but ends with airships scattered by high winds. Five are lost, including *L.49*, brought down by Nieuports of *escadrille* N152 and captured by the French, and *L.50*, which vanishes over the Mediterranean.

1918

21 March	German *'Kaiserschlacht'* offensive begins with Operation *Michael*.
1 April	RFC and RNAS combine into Royal Air Force.
12-20 July	*L.54* and *L.60* are bombed in their shed at Tondern, in southern Denmark, by six Sopwith 2F1 Camels launched from the aircraft carrier HMS *Furious* during Operation *F.7*.
5 August	In the last Zeppelin attack on Britain, *L.70* is destroyed off Norfolk by DH 4 A8032, crewed by Majs Egbert Cadbury and Robert Leckie; Frgkpt Peter Strasser is among the 22 Germans killed.
11 August	*L.53* is destroyed by Sopwith 2F1 Camel N6812 flown by Lt S. D. Culley, launched from lighter *H5* towed by the destroyer HMS *Redoubt*.

DESIGN AND DEVELOPMENT

ZEPPELIN

On 18 August 1863, Ferdinand *Graf* von Zeppelin, a Württemberger with an engineering degree who was visiting the United States as a military observer amid its Civil War, took time off from inspecting the latest developments in the Union Army to take a unique view of Minnesota from a captive hydrogen balloon owned by German immigrant John H. Steiner. 'While I hovered over St Paul', Zeppelin wrote in a letter to his father afterward, 'the idea of air navigation struck me'.

That conceptual seed, combined with his observations of the French use of free-floating balloons to maintain communication with the outside world during the Siege of Paris in 1870, spurred Zeppelin on a quest for a means of propelling and controlling lighter-than-air craft. His efforts finally bore fruit during the afternoon of 2 July 1900, when the first of his giant motorized airships, containing hydrogen in gas cells within a rigid aluminium alloy framework, lifted off from its floating hangar on Lake Constance. Among the observers of *LZ.1*'s historic 17-minute flight were members of the German Ministry of Defence, whose first impression fixated on its speed of 5.5 metres per second, which they judged too slow to be of military use.

The majestic airship had caught the public imagination, however, and further development led to increases in size, range, altitude, carrying capacity and speed. *LZ.4*, first flown on 20 June 1908, was 446ft long, 42ft 6in in diameter, contained 17 gas cells and was powered by two 105hp Daimler engines that gave it a top speed of 30mph. On 1 July, it made a 12-hour flight from Lake Constance to Zürich, Switzerland, and back. Engine problems during a flight on 4 August forced the airship down at Echterdingen, where a gas leak and a static spark caused *LZ.4* to burn before more than 40,000 appalled spectators, but unsolicited public donations raised six million marks to allow Zeppelin to continue his work.

On 8 September, the *Luftschiffbau* Zeppelin gmbh was established at Friedrichshafen and on 10 November Kaiser Wilhelm II was among 12 passengers aboard an enlarged *LZ.3* as it rose over Lake Constance, thus becoming the first head of state to fly. On 16 November 1909, Zeppelin business manager Alfred Colsman founded the world's first airline, the *Deutsche Luftschifffahrt-Aktiengesellschaft* (DELAG), as a civilian option in case the German military did not adopt the airship. In the three years prior to the start of World War I, the rapidly improving Zeppelins logged an impressive 100,000 miles carrying 37,250 passengers without a mishap. A direct consequence of this success was that airships had found niches in military as well as civilian service by the summer of 1914.

While Zeppelin continued to refine his airship's design after *LZ.4*'s destruction in 1908, that calamity also inspired Professor Johann Schütte to try improving on it with an airship of his own. With the backing of industrialist Dr Karl Lanz, the Schütte-

From left, Dr Hugo Eckener, pre-war collaborator in Zeppelin airship development and wartime trainer of naval airship crews, Ferdinand *Graf* von Zeppelin and Frgtnkpt Peter Strasser had a five-year association. Asked by an American journalist of his moral qualms about his creation's use in bombing cities, Zeppelin replied, 'No one regrets more deeply than I do that non-combatants have been killed, but they have been killed by other weapons of war too'. (Greg VanWyngaden)

'R' TYPE ZEPPELIN

649ft 11in.

61ft 4in.

'R' Type Zeppelin *L.30*, commanded by *Kapitänleutnant* Horst *Freiherr* Treusch von Buttlar-Brandenfels, at Nordholz, Germany, in September 1916. Designed by E. H. L. Dürr, the 'Thirties' class of 'Super Zeppelins' sought to improve their survivability with greater volume, fewer but larger hydrogen cells within lightened airframes and more power from six 240hp Maybach 6-cylinder HSLu engines. With a cruising range of 2,300 miles and an operational ceiling of 17,700ft, it carried up to 22 crewmen and four to five tons of bombs. Commanded by Kptltn von Buttlar-Bandenfels and flying from Nordholz, *L.30*'s first raid on 31 July 1916 was aborted due to bad weather, but it bombed coastal towns on 8–9 August, Bungay in Suffolk on 3 September and east London 20 days later. Clear weather and strong anti-aircraft defence convinced Buttlar-Brandenfels to give London a wide berth on 25 September, deteriorating weather cut short his sortie on 1 October and two engine failures ten minutes after take-off induced him to abort on 27 November. Obsolete by 1918, *L.30* survived to be confiscated by the Inter-Allied Commission after the war.

Lanz *Luftschiffsbau* was formed in Mannheim on 22 April 1909. On 1 October 1911, its first product, *SL.1*, took to the sky at nearby Rheinau. Containing its gas cells within a wirebraced lattice frame of composite wood and plywood, *SL.1* was 430ft long and 60ft in diameter, with power provided by four 500hp Daimler engines.

Subsequent Schütte-Lanz airships outperformed their early Zeppelin counterparts due to a more aerodynamically refined hull shape, and they introduced features that Zeppelin would later adopt, such as cruciform tail surfaces and an enclosed crew gondola. Both armed services purchased Schütte-Lanz ships, but the *Deutsche Luftstreitkräfte* (German Air Force) soon abandoned airships as a weapon, whilst the *Kaiserliche Marine* discovered that in spite of it being coated in casein glue that was in turn lacquered and coated with paraffin, the Schütte-Lanz's frame remained vulnerable to moisture, resulting in adhesive breakdown and a prodigious maintenance headache. 'Most of the Schütte-Lanz ships are not usable under combat conditions', Frgkpt Peter Strasser, commander of the *Kaiserliche Marine*'s airship force, declared, 'especially those operated by the Navy, because their wooden construction cannot cope with the damp conditions inseparable from maritime service'.

BRITISH HOME DEFENCE

In July 1914, Britain officially had two military air arms, the RFC serving the Army and the RNAS under the control of the Admiralty, which in the latter case meant its aggressive First Sea Lord, Winston Churchill, and the commander of its Air Department, the progressive-minded Capt Murray Sueter. In August, while the RFC was committing what aircraft it had to supporting the British Expeditionary Force on the Western Front, the RNAS devoted part of its resources to Home Defence. That included increasing the number of high-angle guns from the 30 with which Britain entered the war and patrolling the most likely approaches from which German aircraft were likely to come.

Completed in Potsdam as *LZ.58* on 14 November 1915, this Zeppelin served the *Deutsches Heer* as *LZ.88*, carrying out 14 reconnaissance missions and three bombing sorties over the Western Front, dropping 9,367lb of bombs. As the *Deutsches Heer* lost confidence in airships, in January 1917 it bequeathed *LZ.88* to the *Kaiserliche Marine*, which conducted tests with it as *L.25* until 15 September, when it was decommissioned and broken up at Potsdam. (Greg VanWyngarden)

LUFTFAHRZEUGBAU SCHÜTTE-LANZ · MANNHEIM-RHEINAU

Zeichnung von Prof. Hans Rud. Schulze

A postcard depiction of a Schütte-Lanz airship, whose wooden structure soon lost favour against the Zeppelin's Duralumin, but whose general configuration influenced the later, more refined Zeppelin designs. (Greg VanWyngarden)

OVERLEAF
2Lt William Leefe Robinson of No. 39 (Home Defence) Sqn became the first airman to destroy an enemy airship over England during the early hours of 3 September 1916, for which he was awarded the Victoria Cross. Robinson, flying BE 2c 2693 from Sutton's Farm in Essex, established a formula for 'Zepp strafing' when, after raking his target's underside with two magazines of incendiary ammunition without result, he concentrated his third and last drum in one small area. He was rewarded with a pink glow within the airship, then flames that towered 100ft high as the wooden-framed Schütte-Lanz airship SL.11 plunged to earth near Cuffley, killing Hptm Wilhelm Schramm and his 15 crewmen.

On 5 September, Churchill announced a three-tier defence plan. RNAS units in France would strike at airship bases within reach, a second line of aircraft would patrol an arc covering the airspace between Dover and London, and RNAS pilots based at Hendon would constitute the third and final defensive line. Aeroplanes in 1914 had a slow rate of climb, but information relayed from the first line of defence would give those in the remaining two lines time to ascend to the airships' height, while the first-line aeroplanes would be ready to engage the enemy on their return flight.

BE 2c

27ft 3in.

2693

36ft 10in.

On 1 October, blackout instructions were inaugurated throughout England, and on the 9th the RNAS formed the Anti-Aircraft Corps, mobilizing part-time volunteers to man the guns and searchlights. October also saw the RNAS request RFC assistance in Home Defence, starting with the deployment of two aeroplanes of No. 1 Sqn to Hounslow in west London and two to Joyce Green near Dartford in Kent.

By December, lighting restrictions were in effect in London, with coastal towns and cities in the Midlands soon following suit. The RNAS had about 40 land aeroplanes at 12 stations along the east coast, from Killingholme in north Lincolnshire to Dover in Kent, as well as 20 seaplanes on standby.

Churchill and Sueter, agreeing from the onset that the best defence was a good offence, launched a series of pre-emptive strikes at Zeppelin bases. After No. 3 Wing was transferred from Eastchurch in Kent to the Belgian port city of Antwerp, two of its aircraft attacked the Zeppelin sheds at Cologne and two others those at Düsseldorf on 22 September. Only one 20lb bomb hit the target and results were negligible. On 8 October, however, Flt Lt Reginald L. G. Marix, flying Sopwith Tabloid 168, bombed and destroyed the newest army Zeppelin, *Z.IX*, in its Düsseldorf shed. On 21 November, three RNAS Avro 504s flew from Belfort to bomb Zeppelin's very centre at Friedrichshafen, but again damage was slight.

By Christmas Eve, when Oblt-z-S Stefan von Prondzynski in a Friedrichshafen FF 29 floatplane of *See Flieger Abteilung* 1

In March 1916, Zeppelins began using the Goerz *Spähgondel* or *Spähkorb*. Developed by Paul Jaray, it could be lowered as much as 3,280ft below the airship – and the clouds. The lone observer had a wicker chair, chart table, electric lamp, compass, lightning conductor and a telephone connected via a brass insulated core within the steel cable – it was also the only place on the airship where he could smoke! Peter Strasser was never convinced of its usefulness, however, and sub-cloud cars, as the Allies called them, were used only on *Deutsches Heer* airships. (Christophe Cony)

A Goldschmidt incendiary bomb, preserved at the *Musée de l'Air et l'Espace*, contained a mixture of Benzol, tar and Thermite under an outer casing of tarred rope. A three-foot calico streamer served as its only stabilizer. (Christophe Cony)

dropped the first bomb on British soil – a 22 'pounder' that missed its target, Dover Castle in Kent, and slightly wounded two men at nearby St James Rectory – the British Army had taken over London's anti-aircraft defence. It had by then deployed a growing number of 3in guns and searchlights ringing important urban centres throughout the country. On Christmas Day, the Royal Navy struck again as three channel packets converted into seaplane carriers – HMS *Empress*, *Riviera* and *Engadine* – with some 100 warships milling about the North Sea in readiness to protect them, despatched seven Short floatplanes, carrying three 20lb bombs each, to attack targets in and around Cuxhaven, including the Zeppelin sheds at nearby Nordholz. Little damage was done, but this imaginative air-sea raid set a precedent for combined arms operations to come.

TECHNICAL
SPECIFICATIONS

'P' AND 'R' CLASS ZEPPELINS

The principal Zeppelin airship when war broke out was the 'M' class, but the quest for more battle-worthy performance was swift in coming. On 5 August 1914, the Zeppelin company gave the Navy Ministry a proposal for a new, enlarged 'P' class, originally conceived as a passenger carrier for DELAG, but now with military roles in mind. Based on *LZ.26*, it was the first to use a framework of Duralumin – an alloy of aluminium and four per cent copper that was considerably lighter than pure aluminium – with a keel inside the structure. Between 17 girders, 60ft in diameter, were 16 gas cells, usually made from three layers of goldbeater's skin (an impermeable parchment made from the outer membrane of a calf's stomach – with anywhere from 50,000 to 80,000 animals being sacrificed per airship, accounting for much of its expense) glued over a cotton backing, though later wartime shortages necessitated the use of heavier rubberized cotton instead. Automatic pressure release valves were installed below each cell, but there were no trunking outlets, the released hydrogen simply drifting upward and diffusing out of the hull, whose upper surfaces were left undoped.

The 'P' class was more streamlined than its predecessors, with 197ft of its 536ft 5in length being parallel sided. Its greater volume gave it the ability to fly farther and higher and carry a heavier payload, and the crew was afforded the relative comfort of fully enclosed gondolas. It also had a fourth engine (the 'M' class had

This view of the control gondola for Schütte-Lanz *SL.14* shows a layout not far removed from a Zeppelin's. Powered by four 240hp Maybach engines, the 571ft long *SL.14* was operated by the *Kaiserliche Marine* from Seerappen and Wainoden, flying two reconnaissance missions and two bombing raids over northern Russia before damage led to it being scrapped on 18 May 1917. (Steve Suddaby)

only three), raising its top speed to 63mph – 11mph quicker than the previous model.

The first 'P' class Zeppelin, *LZ.38*, was delivered to the *Deutsche Luftstreitkräfte* on 3 April 1915. By then, however, the *Kaiserliche Marine* was already requesting an improved class of airship from both Zeppelin and Schütte-Lanz that could operate from existing sheds. This was subsequently rejected in favour of an enlarged six-engined airship, which would be accommodated within larger sheds. The double sheds at Tondern and Seddin were lengthened, four giant sheds were built anew at Ahlhorn and a new, larger assembly shed was built at the Zeppelin factory at Friedrichshafen, in addition to which a new Zeppelin factory was built at Staaken, near Berlin.

Produced with the aid of aerodynamicist Paul Jaray, the 'R' class airships were larger and abandoned the parallel lines of their 'P' and similar 'Q' class predecessors for a more streamlined curvature along the hull. They became mainstays of the climactic bombing raids of 1916, and the capture of *L.33* on 24 September 1916 allowed the British to document their construction in detail, giving posterity its best glimpse of a characteristic wartime Zeppelin airship.

Airship class	'P' (LZ.38)	'R' (L.30)
Power	6 x 6-cylinder 240hp Maybach 3M C-X	6 x 6-cylinder 240hp Maybach HSLu
Length	536ft 5in	649ft 11in
Max diameter	61ft 4in	78ft 5in
Gas capacity	1,162,400 cu ft	1,949,600 cu ft
Armament	7–8 x 8mm Maxim-Nordenfelt machine guns 4,400lb bombs	4 x 8mm Maxim-Nordenfelt machine guns 8,000–10,000lb bombs
Max speed	57mph	62.6mph
Service Ceiling	11,700ft	17,700ft
Crew	19	22

INSIDE THE ENVELOPE

Under the cellulose acetate doped cotton fabric that covered the 'R' Zeppelin's hull was a framework of 20 13-sided Duralumin frames, the largest having a diameter of 78ft 6in, braced by radial and chordwise hard-drawn carbon steel cables. These were held together by longitudinal Duralumin girders of isosceles triangular cross section and a lengthwise axial cable or *Zentralverspannung*, the first of its kind used in a Zeppelin. The transverse polygonal rings were 32ft 9in apart (save for the two foremost, which were spaced at 26ft 2in intervals), with 19 unbraced intermediate rings installed between them.

The longitudinal girders included one upper and two lower ones of a 'W' section double structure, since they were the most heavily loaded. Between them and the lesser longitudinals, they gave the airship's hull a 25-sided polygonal appearance. The Duralumin girders weighed only eight pounds per foot, yet a 17ft section withstood loads of up to 10,000lb before collapsing. Extending from the longitudinals at the rear were four rigidly braced vertical and horizontal stabilizers, with rudders and elevators controlled by two cables running along the lower part of the keel.

The keel itself consisted of two large girders of triangular section. An additional pair of box girders 31ft below the top of the keel amidships supported the bombs, fuel tanks, water ballast bags and a one-foot-wide plywood catwalk without guard rails. Externally, the keel supported the gondola strut attachments, mooring points and handling rope connections.

In spite of rubberized tape on the cable ends, the maze of cables inevitably caused tears in the cells, making their maintenance a frequent in-flight affair. 'Rents less than four feet long and triangular tears and patches up to 18in or two feet can be repaired during flight', said *L.33*'s captured sailmaker under interrogation. 'The repair is carried out simply by gathering up the slack of the gas bag round the hole and tying it off'. Rubberized fabric patches using rubber solution could cover smaller holes.

The hydrogen – produced by passing steam over hot iron – had to be carefully pumped into the cells and checked for purity, and all components then checked for leakage, since contamination by anywhere from six to 90 per cent air rendered it explosive. Even after all repairs, filling, refuelling and inspections, a Zeppelin remained in its shed for at least 24 hours before being cleared for a mission.

Each of the airship's 19 gas cells had an automatic valve for releasing hydrogen, while 11 had hand-operated manoeuvring valves that could be actuated from the control gondola. Another 'R' ship innovation was five ventilation shafts leading from the main catwalk to the upper hull, with wooden cowls protecting them from the weather and venting them to the rear. Fourteen rubberized cloth ballast bags held 2,200lb of water and glycerine antifreeze that could be discharged through aluminium pipes when the airship needed to be lightened. There were originally 54 drum-shaped Duralumin 'slip tanks', each containing about 64 gallons of fuel, but that was later reduced to 30. These were suspended by cable, with a slip-release bolt allowing them to be jettisoned if need be. Fuel was pumped by hand from them to 148-gallon gravity tanks located above each engine, along with oil and water tanks.

Bombs were suspended vertically from racks amidships and dropped through a shutter that was slid out of their way. In its last raid, *L.33* carried four 660lb bombs,

L.49's captain used a ship-like telegraph to transmit his orders to the engineers and crew. (Christophe Cony)

ZEPPELIN ARMAMENT

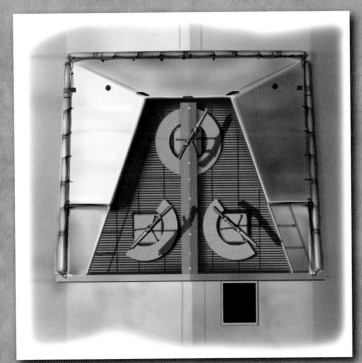

While *Deutsches Heer* airships defended themselves with 7.92mm Parabellum machine guns, those flown by the *Kaiserliche Marine* carried 8mm Maxims as depicted here – the only water-cooled machine guns to see aerial service. In respect to offensive armament, Zeppelins typically carried a mixed load of Carbonit bombs in 22, 110, 220 and 660lb sizes. Incendiary bombs (containing a mixture of Benzol, tar and Thermite beneath an outer casing of tarred rope) were also routinely used, these being stabilized by a three-foot calico streamer.

40 of 128lb each and 60 25lb incendiaries. Defensive armament included an upper gun platform of 0.32in corrugated Duralumin sheet supporting three tripod-mounted 8mm Maxim-Nordenfeldt machine guns, each fed by two Duralumin boxes of 250 armour-piercing and explosive rounds each. The crew reached it by climbing through an internal access shaft and communicated with the control gondola by voicepipe, a special whistle or two gongs worked by cables. Aft of the upper rudder, another machine gunner climbed a sloping ladder to occupy a plywood platform covered in cotton fabric. He communicated with the control gondola by telegraph unless a situation in which sparks would constitute a hazard necessitated it being disconnected.

'HEIGHT CLIMBERS'

The sudden surge in airship losses over England in the last few months of 1916 put their practicality into serious doubt. The *Deutsche Luftstreitskräfte* abandoned them altogether, reviving its bombing campaign against the enemy's homeland using twin-engined Gotha bombers and *Riesenflugzuege* (giant aeroplanes) powered by anywhere from three to five engines. The *Kaiserliche Marine*, equally appalled, would have likewise vetoed continuing its Zeppelin campaign had it not been for Peter Strasser's insistence that they still were still of value, regardless of the direct material damage done, due to 'the general result of the German onslaught upon England's insularity otherwise undisturbed by war'.

Britain's own official air history supported his argument:

By the end of 1916 there were specifically retained in Great Britain for home anti-aircraft defence 17,341 officers and men. There were 12 Royal Flying Corps squadrons, comprising approximately 200 officers, 2000 men and 110 aeroplanes. The anti-aircraft guns and searchlights were served by 12,000 officers and men who would have found a ready place, with continuous work, in France or other war theatres.

Still, the improvements in British Home Defence fighters had to be addressed, and the German Admiralty's Aviation Department suggested steps to improve the airship's speed, such as more streamlined gondolas and paired Maybach engines driving a single propeller with more efficiency than the three-engine car and outrigger brackets of the current crop of Zeppelins. Development delays in the twin-engined drive prevented those airships from entering service, but on 17 January 1917, Strasser proposed another means of eluding enemy interceptors – outclimbing them.

At a conference ten days later, a special commission was formed to oversee improvements that would raise the Zeppelin's operational ceiling. These included a twin-engined rear gondola with two engines driving a single propeller, a fuel reduction from 36 to 30 hours' worth, a 50 per cent reduction in bomb release mechanisms (eight for 660lb bombs, 16 for 200lb bombs and 60 for incendiaries), removal of all defensive armament, a lightened hull structure, a more compact control car and the elimination of crew's quarters and comforts. Even the goldbeater's skin for the hydrogen cells was reduced from three layers to two.

Back at Nordholz, Strasser saw that these modifications were made on *Luftschiffe L.35, L.36, L.39* and *L.40*. Testing yielded unprecedented altitudes of up to 17,700ft, which, in spite of crew complaints of slight dizziness and mild palpitations at those

This 'Cloud Car' was unmanned when *LZ.90*'s winch went out of control and it fell to earth in England on the night of 3 September 1916. (Imperial War Museum Q 31460)

heights, encouraged Strasser to order a new generation of 'Height Climbers'. The first of this 'S' class, *L.42*, was delivered on 28 February, and in a test flight on 10 March with Kptltn Martin Dietrich at the helm and Strasser aboard, it reached 19,700ft. Along with the technical improvements, *L.42* introduced a coat of black dope over all but the upper portion of the hull to render it less conspicuous to ground observers at night.

On 21 August, *L.53* inaugurated the 'V' class Zeppelin, with the nine largest frames spaced 49ft 2in apart rather than 32ft 8in, silk in place of cotton fabric and a tightly doped outer skin to reduce friction. In April 1918, Strasser reconsidered his decision regarding armament and restored gun platforms aboard *L.43* and *L.44*, while pressing for development of the Becker 20mm cannon for airship defence.

Although capable of reaching 20,700ft, *L.53*'s lightened frame was more fragile, limiting its ability to manoeuvre. Moreover, the rarified atmosphere in which the 'Height Climbers' were expected to operate reduced motor efficiency to as low as 50 per cent. The higher altitudes also introduced new difficulties in predicting the high winds that the airships might encounter. Such conditions could easily prove dangerous to crews who had little experience of strong sub-stratospheric winds and currents that meteorological forecasters at the Hamburg Observatory were unable to predict. Furthermore, navigation at such heights rendered landmarks indistinct, especially at night, making the Zeppelin commanders dependent upon radio guidance from their shore stations – which could be picked up by the British, allowing them to pinpoint their positions.

Besides extreme cold that could be relieved only by more layers of clothing, airship crewmen had to endure the rarified oxygen, which above 12,000ft brought on 'altitude sickness'. Individual bottles of oxygen were issued and their use generally made mandatory above 16,000ft, but their contents were often impure and their side effects ranged from stomach pains to cracked lips. Dewar flasks of liquid air replaced them later in the war.

Airship type	'V' (L.53)	'X' (L.70)
Power	6 x 6-cylinder 240hp Maybach HSLu	7 x 7-cylinder 260hp Maybach MBIVa
Length	644ft 8in	693ft 11in
Gas capacity	1,997,360 cu ft	2,195,800 cu ft
Armament	4 x 8mm Maxim-Nordenfelt machine guns 8,000lb bombs	1 x 20mm Becker cannon 3 x 8mm Maxim-Nordenfelt machine guns 8,000lb bombs
Useful lift	89,500lb	97,130lb
Max speed	66mph	81mph
Service Ceiling	20,700ft	23,000ft

Until aeroplanes came into their own, anti-aircraft guns guided by searchlights constituted the backbone of British air defence. A mainstay from 1915 on was the 13lb 9cwt anti-aircraft gun, here shown mounted on a Thornycroft Type J lorry in France. (Greg VanWyngarden)

BRITISH HOME DEFENCE

Although AAA and searchlights constituted the most consistent weapons against Zeppelin raids, it was aeroplanes that caught the public attention at home – much as they had over the Western Front. The publicity heaped on their first successes did much to reassure British civilians that progress was being made toward their safety. The unique nature of the nocturnal, high-flying hydrogen-filled airships spurred the development of some equally peculiar aeroplanes and weapons for countering them, yet the plurality of air-to-air successes at the most critical juncture of the struggle were accomplished by a thoroughly conventional aircraft which, even at the time, seemed the very antithesis of a fighter.

BE 2c NIGHTFIGHTER

Developed in the autumn of 1911 by superintendent Mervyn O'Gorman and engineers Geoffrey de Havilland and F. M. Green at the Royal Aircraft Factory (RAF) at Farnborough in Hampshire, the 'Blériot Experimental' BE 1 was, in spite of its designation, an original design – and the first aeroplane built from the onset for military use, as opposed to an adapted civilian aircraft. Advanced for its time, the BE 1 was a biplane with no wing stagger or dihedral, wing warping for lateral control and a 60hp Wolseley engine driving a four-bladed tractor propeller to a maximum speed of 59mph.

Flight tested by de Havilland on New Year's Day 1912, the BE 1 became the model for a series of reconnaissance aeroplanes of which some 3,500 would be built, mostly by sub-contractors. The principal types in the summer of 1914 were the BE 2, BE 2a and BE 2b, all powered by 70hp Renault V8 engines that increased their speed to 65mph at 6,500ft, climbed to 7,000ft in 35 minutes and gave the biplanes a three-hour endurance.

From their inception, BEs were involved in advancing the state of the art of military aviation. In January 1912, a wireless set devised by R. Widdington, who had joined the RAF from Cambridge University, was installed in the BE 1, which was then flown by de Havilland, with Capt H. P. T. Lefroy of the Royal Engineers as his observer, to conduct the first successful wireless-directed artillery shoot over Salisbury Plain. In May, Lefroy installed a generator for the wireless, driven by the BE 1's engine via a length of bicycle chain. On 12 August, a BE 2 set a British altitude record at 10,560ft.

2Lt William Leefe Robinson's BE 2c provides some nightfighter cockpit details. The three buttons on the right side of the rear cockpit activated the wingtip and tail navigation lights. Twelve very light signal cartridges can be seen below and to the left of the compass. The fabric-sided windscreen was collapsible so the Lewis gun could be lowered for reloading without cracking the glass. (Greg VanWyngarden)

When war broke out, BE 2a 347 of No. 2 Sqn, flown by Lt Hubert D. Harvey-Kelly, was the first RFC aeroplane to land in France on 3 August 1914. Twenty-two days later, Lts Harvey-Kelly and W. H. C Mansfield attacked a Rumpler Taube with pistols, forced it to land and, after unsuccessfully pursuing its crew into the nearby woods, returned to set it on fire and took off for home. They were duly credited with the RFC's first 'aerial victory'. On 26 April 1915, BE 2b 687 of No. 2 Sqn flew 35 miles to drop a 100lb bomb on the railway junction at Kortrijk in Belgium. Struck in the thigh, abdomen and hand by ground fire, 2Lt William B. Rhodes-Moorhouse managed to bring his aeroplane in with some 95 holes in it and subsequently wrote up a full report on the mission *before* going to the casualty clearing station. He died of his wounds the next day. Shortly afterward, Rhodes-Moorhouse became the first airman to be awarded the Victoria Cross.

Meanwhile, Edward Teshmaker Busk had joined the Royal Aircraft Factory and conducted experiments in stability, which led to the 'reconnaissance experimental' RE 1 before he applied his findings to the BE airframe. The result was a new wing with a 3.5-degree dihedral, front stagger to alter the centre of gravity and a set of four ailerons, as well as a rectangular horizontal stabilizer and a triangular vertical fin in front of the rudder. The resultant BE 2c made its first flight on 30 May 1914, and while flying it to Salisbury Plain on 9 June, Maj William Sefton Brancker claimed that once he reached the cruising altitude of 2,000ft he did not need to touch the controls for the next 40 miles. The first Vickers-built BE 2c arrived on 19 December. By that time, ironically, Busk had been killed on 5 November, his BE 2c having caught fire in the air.

Mainly powered by the 90hp RAF 1a engine, BE 2cs were also fitted with the 105hp RAF 1b and 1d, the 70hp Renault and various Hispano-Suizas. Some of the 300 BE 2cs used by the RNAS for bombing, anti-submarine patrol and training duties had 90hp Curtiss OX-5s.

Besides reconnaissance, the RFC used the BE 2c as a bomber by fairing over the front cockpit to accommodate two 112lb bombs in place of the observer. As aerial combat became more frequent, Capt Louis A. Strange devised a pipe type mount for a Lewis machine gun, which the observer could remove and reinstall in several different locations around his cockpit. Manhandling the weapon about and aiming it through the struts and wires was awkward enough in encounters with German two-seaters, but when the nimble Fokker E I single-seat fighter with its synchronized forward-firing machine gun appeared over the Western Front in August 1915, the 'Strange mount' was hopelessly outclassed. This in turn made the BE 2 the very embodiment of what the British called 'Fokker fodder'.

When the Zeppelin raids began, the RNAS deployed some of its BE 2cs for Home Defence duties in July 1915. In October, two were stationed at Northolt in Middlesex, two at Hainault Farm and two at Sutton's Farm in Essex. In December, seven aerodromes around London were instructed to have two BE 2cs manned by pilots trained in night-fighting. In this role, the BE 2c's fabled stability, which had become such a liability against enemy fighters, became an asset again, reducing the risks of night flying and providing a stable gun platform. BE 2cs and later BE 2es

slated for Home Defence had a Lewis gun on a Strange mount adjusted to fire upward.

In the summer of 1915, Cdr Neville F. Usborne and Lt Cdr de Courcy W. P. Ireland experimented with suspending a BE 2c beneath an SS-type airship, where it would hang until a Zeppelin was sighted. The pilot would then use quick-release devices to drop from the envelope, start the engine and attack. In August 1915, Flt Cdr W. C. Hicks conducted preliminary trials at RNAS Kingsnorth in Kent, but reported control weaknesses that required modifications. Usborne and Ireland crewed the 'airship-plane' in its second trial on 21 February 1916, but at 4,000ft it exceeded its equilibrium weight, causing airship AP 1 to lose gas pressure and buckle. The forward suspension cable parted, dropping the BE 2c's nose and throwing Ireland out. The overloaded rear cables then sheared and the aeroplane sideslipped and crashed into Strood railway station, killing Usborne as well. The 'airship-plane' concept died with its creators.

Even struggling up from the ground, BE 2cs proved surprisingly successful at intercepting Zeppelins. The first opportunity came on 31 March 1916, when 2Lt Albert de Bathe Brandon of No. 39 (Home Defence) Sqn overtook the crippled *L.15* near Brentwood. After dropping Ranken darts and an incendiary bomb on the target, Brandon lost sight of it, but about an hour later *L.15* broke its back and came down in the sea near Knock Deep, east of the Thames Estuary. Ground defences were probably more responsible for *L.15*'s demise, but six months later the Home Defence BE 2c pilots – including Brandon – would come into their own with a vengeance.

RANKEN DART

Until a technique for using incendiary machine gun ammunition was perfected, the British tried various weapons to attack German airships from above – provided their aeroplanes could get above them. In 1915, the pilot would drop a 10 or 20lb Cooper or Hales bomb, which, for want of racks, had to be carried in his lap, with all the attendant hazards involved. In April 1916, the RAF produced 12 Fiery Grapnels for testing. Carried in twos between the undercarriage legs, the grapnels were dropped so their four barbs would tear through the fabric and a 'striker', activated by the pressure of the fabric on a pair of arms sticking out either side, would set off a tongue of flame for 60 seconds to ignite the escaping hydrogen. During testing, however, the grapnels were found to be difficult to deploy and the aeroplane could seldom get high enough above the airship to drop them effectively.

Lt Cdr Francis Ranken's explosive dart consisted of a nine-inch-long tinplate tube with a cast iron point at one end and three spring arms topped by a cap at the other. Dropped in batches of three above the airship, the darts penetrated the fabric and when some 18in within the airship, any of three extending spring arms touched off a spark-producing black powder charge in the tail. Carried 24 tubes to a box, which was fitted to incline 40 degrees down and aft on the floor of the BE 2c's fuselage, the Ranken darts saw some use, mainly by the RNAS, but were not regarded highly because damp conditions often affected the phosphorus inside them.

Home Defence units experimented with wing-mounted French Le Prieur rockets against balloons, but their 50-yard range and gross inaccuracy rendered them virtually useless against a moving airship. The most successful anti-Zeppelin weapon ultimately proved to be the Lewis machine gun using incendiary or explosive ammunition, such as the SPK Mk VIIT 'Sparklet', the Brock, the Pomeroy PSA Mk II and the Buckingham Mk VII, usually in a combined mix.

BE 2c	
Engine	90hp RAF 1a eight-cylinder air-cooled engine
Wingspan (upper)	36ft 10in
Wing area	371 sq ft
Chord (upper wing)	4ft 11in
Chord (lower wing)	3ft 4in
Dihedral	3.5 degrees
Length	27ft 3in
Height	11ft 4in
Armament	1 x 0.303in Lewis machine gun
	Ranken darts
	Incendiary bombs

ZEPP-HUNTERS, SPECIALIZED OR OTHERWISE

Although the BE 2c logged a remarkable record of success against German airships, a wide variety of aircraft designs were considered for dealing with the threat, some adapted to the task as the BE had been and some specially designed for Zeppelin-hunting alone. Ironically, while some of them incorporated interesting and even advanced features, none of the specialized Zepp-hunters achieved production, let alone success.

PUSHERS

The RFC had used pusher fighters since the Vickers FB 5, RAF FE 2 and Aircraft Manufacturing Company (Airco) DH 2, all designed in 1915. In that same year, Harris Booth of the Admiralty Air Department came up with a specialized biplane pusher for intercepting airships, the AD Scout, as well as the similar Blackburn

The AD Scout represented one of numerous attempts at creating a specialized airship interceptor, none of which improved on the modified BE 2c. Someone among the RNAS personnel examining the prototype seems to have opinions regarding its suitability that he cannot suppress! (Greg VanWyngarden)

Of similar design to the AD Scout, the Blackburn Triplane went the way of most three-winged fighters, save for the Sopwith and the Fokker. (Philip Jarrett collection)

Triplane. Both mounted a single Lewis machine gun in a nacelle at least 10ft above the ground, both were as ungainly to fly as they looked and both were ultimately abandoned as unacceptable.

Two later two-seat pushers were the RAF's Night-flying Experimental 1 and the Vickers FB 25, both powered by Hispano-Suiza engines, and which would have carried two Lewis guns or a Vickers Crayford rocket gun, as well as searchlights. Six NE 1s were built, despite the type's first test flight on 8 September 1917 yielding a slow rate of climb and an inadequate service ceiling of 17,500ft. The sole FB 25, whose nacelle accommodated the pilot and observer-gunner side-by-side, was likewise dismissed as unsatisfactory even before it crashed during testing at Martlesham Heath in Suffolk in May 1917.

KITTENS

In 1916, the Admiralty issued a requirement for a small single-seat biplane, armed with a single 0.303in Lewis machine gun mounted on the upper wing centre section, capable of taking off from a platform on the forecastle of a warship to intercept airships. Prototypes for these diminutive fighters were built at the Port Victoria Marine Aircraft Experimental Depot on the Isle of Grain in Kent and at RNAS Special Experimental Flight at nearby Eastchurch on the Isle of Sheppey.

Designed by W. H. Sayers, the PV 7 Grain Kitten was powered by a geared 45hp ABC Gnat two-cylinder engine. First flying in June 1917, it proved to be tail-heavy and performed poorly. Lt Gilbert H. Millar, chief technical officer at Eastchurch, designed the larger, heavier PV 8, called the Eastchurch Kitten. Powered by a 35hp ungeared Gnat engine – since the geared one was unavailable – and first flown on

7 September 1917, it was initially unstable, but after modifications performed and handled better than the Grain Kitten. Nevertheless, neither aeroplane could overcome the Gnat engine's inherent unreliability and they failed to enter production.

On 13 March 1918, an order was issued to ship the Eastchurch Kitten to the United States for evaluation. Whether or not it actually got there is uncertain, but it seems to have inspired at least one American, James V. Martin, to provide the US Army Air Service (USAS) with a Zeppelin-hunting 'Kitten' of its own. The J. V. Martin K III was of similar configuration to its British predecessors, but with Martin's patented K-shaped struts on the wings, sprung wheels on a semi-retractable undercarriage, ailerons that pivoted externally at the upper wingtips, an oxygen cylinder and an electrical outlet into which the pilot could plug a heated suit (curiously, though, no armament was ever installed). All these innovations, which brought the aeroplane's weight up to 582lb, were to be borne into the air by a 45hp ABC Gnat engine that Martin claimed would give it a maximum speed of 135mph at sea level and 97mph at 25,000ft. During preliminary attempts, however, the prototype climbed no higher than ground effect.

By the time the K III was evaluated at McCook airfield, Ohio, in December 1918, the war and the Zeppelin threat were long past, and the USAS refused to test fly it, declaring its K-strut wing cellule structurally unsound. Though nothing more than an aerial curiosity, the J. V. Martin 'Kitten' somehow survived to be stored in the Smithsonian Institution's Paul Garber facility at Silver Hill, Maryland, where it awaits eventual restoration.

INTERCEPTORS AND LOITERERS

In February 1916, Britain's aerial defence was divided up between the services, with the RNAS responsible for attacking enemy aircraft approaching Britain and the RFC dealing with any that reached the isles. In an early response to the Admiralty's

The Port Victoria PV 7 Grain Kitten was designed by W. H. Sayers in 1917 in response to an Admiralty requirement issued the previous year for a small single-seat biplane, armed with a single 0.303in Lewis machine gun mounted on the upper wing centre section, capable of taking off from a platform on the forecastle of a warship to intercept airships. The aeroplane was soon found to be tail-heavy and its high-lift wings proved unsuitable on such a small design, on top of which its 45hp ungeared ABC Gnat engine was chronically unreliable. (Philip Jarrett collection)

The rival PV 8 Kitten was created by Lt Gilbert H. Millar, chief technical officer at the RNAS Special Experimental Flight at Eastchurch. Although the aeroplane was initially found to be unstable, a redesign flew better than the Grain Kitten. However, as with the PV 7, its unreliable Gnat engine ultimately caused its demise. (Philip Jarrett collection)

requirements, Parnall and Sons built a large biplane, conceived by Keith Davies and realized by Adolf Camden Pratt, with a severe forward stagger and its commodious seat just behind the upper wing for an unobstructed view upward, the lower wing being suspended by struts underneath the shallow fuselage. A single Lewis gun was mounted at an upward angle of 45 degrees slightly to the pilot's right on the upper wing. Powered by a 230hp Sunbeam Maori water-cooled engine, prototype N505 went to Upavon in Wiltshire for testing, but may never have flown. Overweight and judged structurally unsafe during stress testing, the Parnall Scout or 'Zepp-Strafer' was returned to its builder, who burned it along with the drawings and design data.

In the summer of 1916, Vickers produced the FB 11, a large three-seat biplane intended for either anti-airship or long-range escort duties. Designed by R. L. Howard-Flanders, it had a pilot, a rear gunner and another gunner manning a Lewis gun from a nacelle on the upper wing – an arrangement that was already obsolete by the time it was evaluated (Vickers had adopted its own Vickers-Challenger interrupter gear by then). Flying in September and October 1916, and evaluated by the RNAS at Eastchurch in November, it boasted a duration of 7.5 hours, but displayed poor lateral control. Furthermore, its 250hp Rolls-Royce Falcon III V12 engine gave it a disappointing top speed of just 96mph. The aeroplane's destruction in a crash settled the FB 11's fate.

In May 1916, the RNAS examined the possibilities of fitting the American-designed Davis 1½-pound gun, whose explosive shell's recoil was countered by a compensating charge in the rear, in an aircraft. It was a long, unwieldy weapon, but the Admiralty issued a requirement for an aeroplane to carry it for anti-Zeppelin interception. The only response came from Robey Company Ltd of Bracebridge Heath, Lincoln. Designed by J. A. Peters, the Robey-Peters Davis Gun Carrier was a large, cumbersome biplane powered by a 250hp Rolls-Royce engine with two Davis gunners perched in nacelles on the upper wing and the pilot's cockpit sited far aft, his limited vision aided by a transparent panel on either side.

During its first takeoff run at Bracebridge in May 1917, the Robey-Peters' front undercarriage skid and dug into the ground, standing it on its nose. Three days later it took off, but halfway through its circuit the pilot got the aileron controls crossed

and it crashed on the local mental hospital. The pilot was unhurt, but Robey apparently thought this omen enough and burned the prototype.

Early in the war, businessman, politician and RNAS Reservist Noel Pemberton Billing wrote a book, modestly entitled *Air War – How to Wage It*, in which he visualized Britain's skies defended by a fleet of heavily armed aerial cruisers, vigilantly lying in wait for intruders day and night in 12-hour shifts. When Capt Sueter asked for an anti-airship aeroplane in 1915, Billing put his money where his mouth was with the extraordinary PB 29E, a large quadruplane powered by two 90hp Austro-Daimler engines fitted with silencers, driving four-bladed pusher airscrews, which he claimed to have designed and built in only seven weeks. Its Lewis gunner manned his weapon from a nacelle between the two uppermost wings, above two cockpits with dual controls. With only one bay of interplane struts and wire bracing for a biplane running through the two intermediate wings, the aeroplane was structurally fragile. It was tested by Cdr John W. Seddon from Chingford in Essex on 8 February 1916, but crashed shortly thereafter.

In December 1916, Billing sold his interests in Pemberton Billing Ltd to other company directors, and the firm was renamed Supermarine Aviation Works Ltd. With the Admiralty still interested in Billing's Zeppelin-hunter, the quadruplane underwent a redesign, one of the engineers involved being Reginald J. Mitchell, later to design racing aeroplanes and a much more successful Supermarine fighter. The result, grandly designated the PB 31E Night Hawk, was certainly sturdier, with a glazed enclosed cabin for a five-man crew – which in practice could not have exceeded three due to weight considerations – and a sleeping berth for off-duty crewmen. Two 100hp Anzani

The Parnall Scout was meant to destroy Zeppelins, but ended up being destroyed by its own maker. (Philip Jarrett collection)

nine-cylinder air-cooled radial engines drove four-bladed tractor propellers, but the searchlight, flexibly gimbal-mounted in the nose, got its power from a 5hp ABC two-cylinder engine, which also heated the crew compartment – the first auxiliary power unit installed in an aeroplane. Fuel was carried in nine tanks, any of which could be isolated if hit by enemy gunfire. All petrol, air and control leads were armoured. Endurance ranged from nine to 18 hours, with the latter figure achieved by throttling the engines down until the aircraft was flying at just 35mph. Armament was to have been a 1½-pounder Davis gun atop the upper wing, along with two Lewis guns.

Clifford B. Prodger test-flew the PB 31E in February 1917, but its 60mph speed at 6,500ft fell below the 75mph the company predicted. Worse still, its glacial 60-minute climb to 10,000ft would have been hopeless against an airship dropping ballast and escaping upward. As with the J. V. Martin K III, the first Supermarine fighter introduced many components that were ahead of their time, but failed in its primary purpose, and was scrapped on 23 July 1917.

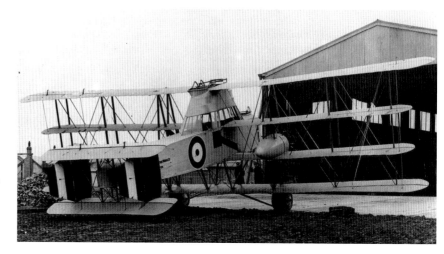

Although it boasted remarkable
technical advances, including the
first auxiliary motor in an
aeroplane, the Supermarine
PB 31 Night Hawk's agonizing rate
of climb made it pathetically
unsuitable for intercepting
Zeppelins. (Philip Jarrett
collection)

STRATEGIC SITUATION

Each of the powers that went to war, one after the other, in the summer of 1914 expected a victorious conclusion by the year's end. By then, however, only one participant could claim to have achieved its strategic objectives – Japan, which, having taken the concession port of Tsingtao in China, was poised to seize most of Germany's Pacific island possessions as well. In contrast, Austria-Hungary, whose invasion of Serbia had touched off the worldwide conflict, had been ignominiously ejected from that country and defeated by the Russians in Galicia. In East Prussia, the Germans had annihilated one Russian army and repulsed another, but on the Western Front their bid to knock France out of the war via neutral Belgium had failed, leaving it facing a resurgent French army, the British Expeditionary Force and a small but determined Belgian army in exile along a line of fortified trenches that extended from the North Sea to the Swiss border.

With the conflict anything but over by Christmas, the now committed powers devoted 1915 to breaking the stalemate. Allied offensives in Artois and Champagne accomplished little. Britain, however, was able to impose a naval blockade on Germany whilst neutralizing the second most powerful high seas fleet on earth. One by one, German cruisers and commerce raiders were eliminated, most notably in the Falklands on 8 December 1914. Closer to home, Royal Navy victories off Heligoland Bight on 28 August 1914 and Dogger Bank on 24 January 1915 discouraged Kaiser Wilhelm from risking the battle fleet whose creation had done so much to turn Britain from a friend into a rival. Even after the epic confrontation off Jutland on 31 May 1916, in which the Royal Navy took a costly tactical beating, the ultimate strategic outcome

was best summarized in the *New York Times* – 'The German fleet has assaulted its jailer, but it is still in jail'.

Stalemate in Europe led to attempts to break the deadlock farther and farther afield. After declaring war on the Ottoman Empire on 2 November 1914, the Russian Caucasus Army, joined by thousands of Armenian volunteers, invaded the Caucasus region. After losing considerable ground, the Ottoman forces managed to contain the offensive by the following summer, and on 24 April 1915, Minister of the Interior Mehmet Talat declared the region's Armenians to be in a state of rebellion and on 27 May ordered their mass deportation to Syria and Mosul – a brutal exodus that would be widely called the Armenian Genocide.

On 3 February, Turkish forces assaulted the British-held Suez Canal, but on the 19th, First Lord of the Admiralty Winston Churchill launched a naval offensive to force the Dardanelles and knock the Ottoman Empire out of the war. When that failed, leading to Churchill's removal from office in May, Allied troops landed at Gallipoli on 25 April, only to be stopped and ultimately compelled to start evacuating on 28 December.

In Africa, German-held Togoland was overrun in 20 days, Kamerun fell on 10 June 1915 and German south-west Africa surrendered on 6 July. That left only German East Africa, but its well-trained native Askari force, brilliantly led by Obstltn Paul von Lettow-Vorbeck, would remain a thorn in the Allies' side for the war's entirety.

Italy entered the war on the Allied side on 23 May 1915, and on 29 June launched its first of four assaults that year against Austro-Hungarian forces along the Isonzo River – each ending in bloody failure. On 3 October, Allied forces landed in Salonika, but on the 6th Austro-Hungarian and German forces plunged into Serbia. On 14 October, Bulgaria entered the war on the side of the Central Powers and helped complete the occupation of Serbia in November, although the Serbian army would fight on in exile in Salonika.

With no dramatic breakthroughs anywhere by the *Deutsches Heer*, and the German populace, feeling the hardships of the British blockade, clamouring for some means of striking back, Germany turned to technology to swing the balance. Kaiser Wilhelm finally authorized the first Zeppelin raid on England on 19–20 January 1915 – many more would follow. On 4 February, the *Kaiserliche Marine* declared its own naval blockade of Britain, relying for its enforcement primarily on its submarines, or *Unterseeboote*, given free reign against Allied and neutral shipping alike. Here, too, the airships played a vital part in the maritime reconnaissance role. When *U-20* sank the liner *Lusitania* off southern Ireland on 7 May, however, the deaths of 128 American passengers aboard the ship led to a protest which resulted in the Kaiser, in an effort to avoid provoking war with the United States, rescinding unrestricted submarine warfare in June.

At Ypres on 22 April, the Germans preceded their assault with clouds of chlorine gas dispensed from canisters along a four-mile front. This initially caused panic among French, Algerian and Canadian troops, but the *Deutsches Heer* failed to take full advantage of it and had insignificant gains to show for it when the Second Battle of Ypres ended on 25 May. What it did accomplish was to start a new arms race as both sides strove to develop filtered masks for the troops' protection, as well as a growing

OPPOSITE

Western Front Zeppelin bases and Home Defence aerodromes, 1915–18.

arsenal of new and more lethal chemical agents. Although chemical warfare would never prove a decisive factor in the war, it added a new dimension of misery for the trench-bound soldiers to endure.

By the end of 1915, Germany was feeling the strain as the British embargo increasingly limited the resources for its war machine and imposed deprivation on its civilian population. For relief it turned to its most effective innovations, the U-boats striking at Allied shipping and the airships that seemed its only means of carrying the war to British soil. For the *Kaiserliche Marine*'s airship commander, Frgkpt Peter Strasser, the use of Zeppelins to strike back and even possibly bring Britain to its knees became literally a lifelong obsession.

THE COMBATANTS

MARINE-LUFTSCHIFF-ABTEILUNG

While the *Kaiserliche Marine* entered the war with only one airship, the *Deutsches Heer* had ten, and these were distributed between the Western and Eastern fronts, initially as scouts in support of the ground troops. This proved to be a serious misuse of what would have been far more useful as high-altitude reconnaissance platforms. On 21 August, the Germans despatched *Z. VII* (redesignated *LZ.22* by the *Deutsches Heer*) and *Z. VIII* (*LZ.23*) to reconnoitre the French army in the Vosges. They found the main army camp, and being only a few hundred feet up, bombed it as well, but the French responded with a barrage of artillery and small-arms fire that riddled both airships. *LZ.22* managed to cross the lines before force landing at Saint-Quirin in Lorraine, but *LZ.23* came down at Bandonvilliers, where its crewmen burned their documents before being captured by French cavalry.

As the war continued, the *Deutsches Heer* used its airships at higher altitudes for both reconnaissance and the bombing campaign, even expending the first bombs on London on 31 May 1915. As the state of the art in aeroplanes advanced concurrent with a rise in airship losses, however, the *Deutsches Heer*'s enthusiasm for them waned, and by the end of 1916 it had largely abandoned the airship in favour of twin-engined Gothas and multi-engined *Riesenflugzeuge*.

The *Kaiserliche Marine*'s *Marine-Luftschiff-Abteilung* (Naval Airship Division), in contrast, rapidly grew through the efforts of two dedicated believers: Konteradmiral Paul Behnke, Deputy Chief of the Naval Staff, and Kvtkpt Peter Strasser. Born in 1876 and a career officer since age 15, Strasser had volunteered for aviation training in 1911 and was offered command of the Airship Division in September 1913. It was Behnke's

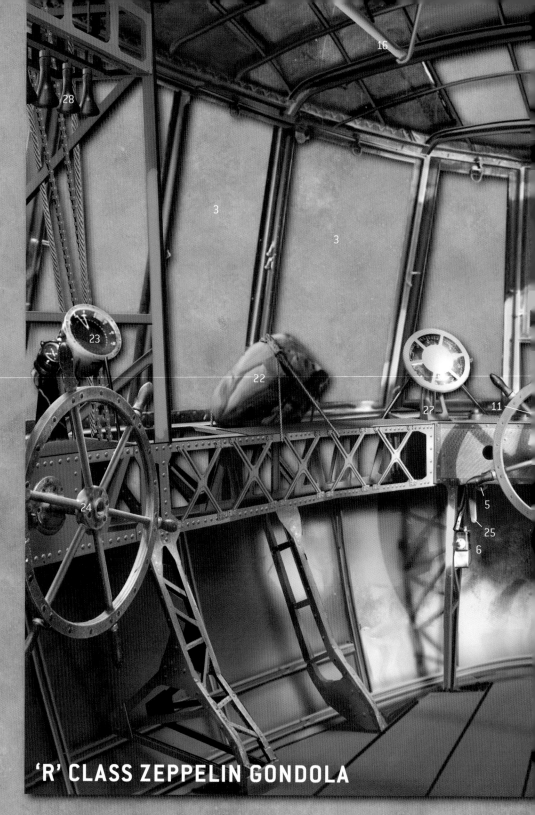

'R' CLASS ZEPPELIN GONDOLA

1. Skylight
2. Triplex glass windscreen
3. Cellon windows
4. Control wheel
5. Cabin lighting
6. Electrical switch
7. Electrical box
8. Control wheel chain
9. Support cables
10. Compass
11. Main instruments
12. Commander's binoculars
13. Oxygen tank
14. Bomb sight
15. Bomb release control panel

16. Grab rails
17. Speaker tube
18. Engine telegraphs
19. Map table
20. Map lamp

21. Storage bins
22. Heineke parachute
23. Altimeter
24. Elevator control wheel
25. Trail and rope handling release

26. Storage cabinet
27. Fuel quantity gauge
28. Ballast release handles

Felix Schwormstadt's depiction of typical activity in a Zeppelin's command gondola was based on Hptm Erich Linnarz and the crew of *LZ.38*, the first to bomb London on 31 May 1915. (Jon Guttman)

persistence that prevailed over the Kaiser's misgivings to gain approval for a bombing campaign against England. Strasser, for his part, energetically expanded the moribund naval arm over which he had been put in charge and, through a combination of strict discipline, intense training and genuine concern for the welfare of his men, instilled a new pride in the division as an elite force. Strasser's unbreakable confidence in the Zeppelin as a weapon prevailed against his superiors' thoughts of disbanding the force, earning him promotions to Fregattenkapitän and, in November 1916, to Führer der Luftschiffe.

Like their seagoing counterparts, giant airships were operated by crews rather than by pilots. Naval Zeppelin *L.33*, which fell into British hands, had 23 men. These consisted of the commander, executive officer, warrant quartermaster (who handled navigation), a warrant engineer, sailmaker (on duty at all times to repair whatever leaks arose), two rudder men, two elevator men, two radio operators and two mechanics for each of the six engines. The doubled enlisted men worked on divided watches, but 'off duty' time tended to be spent at the machine gun positions.

The crew, whether army or navy, had to operate under severe hardships, the most universal of which was freezing temperatures. They wore fur-lined jackets, trousers, gauntlets and helmets, sometimes lent a further layer of insulation with crumpled newspapers, but it never seemed sufficient. Their fur-lined boots had rope soles and were covered with felt overshoes as a further precaution against creating sparks against the Duralumin frame. The engineers worked under slightly warmer conditions, but had to endure exhaust, petrol and oil fumes amid the ear-numbing throb of the Maybach engines.

As some compensation, the airshipmen ate relatively well, with bread, butter, chocolate and tinned hashes or stews that – in obvious lieu of conventional cooking – were heated by means of a chemical process. Hammocks and a ballast bag of drinking water were kept in a plywood-floored 'lounge' area between gas cells. Up to 50 grams of rum or brandy per man might also be carried, depending on the captain's policy. Relief tubes were situated in the gondolas and keel, but gunners could only urinate leeward from their positions, which could eventually rot the adjacent covering. 'R' class Zeppelins introduced a stamped aluminium toilet, but anyone in need in the control gondola faced an 800ft walk to avail himself of that luxury.

While the British branded them 'babykillers', the Germans rationalized their actions as carrying the war over the Channel to a hitherto-complacent enemy who was slowly starving their civilians through the naval blockade. Ernst August Lehmann, who commanded *LZ.17 Sachsen* in both civilian and army capacities, *LZ.XII* and naval airships *LZ.90*, *LZ.98* (*L.52*) and *LZ.120* during the war, wrote in 1927 of the general feeling he observed:

The bitterness of war was increasing almost daily, and as the wounded came back from the front there developed public demand for the most drastic measures against the enemy, particularly France and England. Particularly England, in German eyes, safe across the Channel, must be made to suffer. The best way, according to those who talked the loudest, but who undoubtedly knew least about the subject, was to raze London by fire.

BE 2c COCKPIT

1. Lewis 0.303in machine gun
2. Strange gun mount
3. Collapsible windscreen with fabric side panels
4. Altimeter
5. Airspeed indicator
6. Inclinometer
7. Tachometer
8. Clock
9. Cockpit lighting
10. Slip bubble
11. Air pressure manometer
12. Morse key
13. Wingtip and tail navigation light switches
14. Signal flare cartridges
15. Pilot's seat
16. Control column
17. Spark control lever
18. Rudder bar
19. Primer pump
20. Throttle lever
21. Lewis gun carousels
22. Holt wingtip light switches
23. Compass
24. Flare placard
25. Map
26. Fuel valves

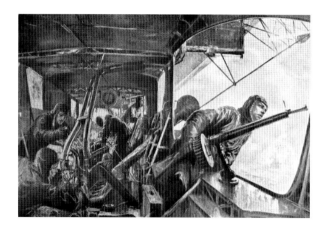

Another Schwormstadt painting captures the tension of the bombing foray from another angle, with a gunner and all crewmen not involved in flying or bombing scanning the sky for enemy aeroplanes. (Greg VanWyngarden)

ROYAL FLYING CORPS

The first unit specifically meant to counter the Zeppelin threat was No. 33 (Home Defence) Sqn, formed on 12 January 1916 under Maj Arthur A. B. Thompson, equipped with FE 2bs and FE 2ds. Its headquarters was at Gainesborough in Lincolnshire, and the unit had flight stations at Brattleby (Scampton) and Kirton-in-Lindsey, both also in Lincolnshire. Prior to that, II Reserve Home Defence Training Squadron had been established at Northolt under Maj B. F. Moore on 1 November 1915. During the course of 1916, No. 33 (Home Defence) Sqn would be joined by Nos. 36, 37, 38, 39, 50, 51, 75, 76, 77 and 78 (Home Defence) Sqns.

In March 1916, London's defences were grouped within No. 18 Wing, under Lt Col Fenton Vesey Holt. Amongst the units under its control was No. 39 (Home Defence) Sqn, which had been created on 15 April 1916 through the redesignation of No. 19 Reserve Aeroplane Sqn. Stationed around London, particularly at Hainault Farm and Sutton's Farm, with its headquarters at Hounslow under the command of Maj Thomas C. R. Higgins, No. 39 (Home Defence) Sqn initially combined training with defence duties. However, in June 1916 its pilots got the welcome news that all Home Defence units would focus on the latter, as part of No. 16 Wing, which from July onward was called Home Defence Wing.

ENGAGING THE ENEMY

By the autumn of 1916, the RFC's Home Defence squadrons had worked out a formula for bringing down Zeppelins with the recently introduced 'Sparklet' tracers, Brock and Pomeroy explosive bullets and Buckingham incendiary rounds, a mix of which was loaded into the magazines of their Lewis machine guns. Tracers helped the pilot to aim at his target, and once he had zeroed in, adjusting his speed and angle of attack to maintain a steady stream of fire into one location, allowing escaping hydrogen to mix with the air until it ignited, the airship's fate was sealed.

The earliest successes in September 1916 were achieved using machine guns with their Strange mountings fixed to fire upward, since the Zeppelins usually reached higher altitudes than the aeroplanes. On 27/28 November, however, 2Lt Ian Vernon Pyott of A Flight, No. 36 (Home Defence) Sqn had his Lewis gun more conventionally mounted above the wing to fire forward on BE 2c 2738 when he scrambled up from Seaton Carew, on the coast of Country Durham, on his second patrol of the night. After an hour he spotted a Zeppelin caught in the Castle Eden searchlight over West Hartlepool and began a circling ascent until he reached 9,800ft.

Pyott's quarry, *L.34*, had just eluded the Hutton Henry searchlight – dropping 13 bombs on it, but scoring no hits – and its captain, Kptnltn der R Max Dietrich (uncle of future film star Marlene Dietrich), chose to press no further inland, dropping another 16 bombs over West Hartlepool before retiring seaward. He had made the fateful error of flying at 9,500ft, giving Pyott the rare opportunity to attack directly from above. The German upper gunners fired back and *L.34* quickly rose. Pyott fired 71 rounds before the airship began to outdistance him, but just as despondency was setting in he saw the hull 'become incandescent' and then burst into flames. Pyott's aeroplane was thrown out of control, but he quickly recovered while *L.34* fell into the sea about 1,800 yards from the Heugh lighthouse at the mouth of the River Tees, killing all 20 of its crew.

Jim Laurier

HORST *FREIHERR* TREUSCH VON BUTTLAR-BRANDENFELS

Horst Julius Ludwig Otto *Freiherr* Treusch von Buttlar-Brandenfels was born in Hanau, in the central German state of Hesse, on 14 June 1888. Upon graduation from school he enlisted in the *Kaiserliche Marine* on 3 April 1907, becoming a Fähnrich-zur-See on 21 April 1908. After serving on a number of warships and rising to the rank of Oberleutnant-zur-See, he entered the *Marine-Luftschiff-Abteilung* as war clouds gathered in 1914. Von Buttlar went on to carry out 221 sorties in Zeppelins *L.6*, *L.11*, *L.30*, *L.25*, *L.54* and *L.72*, including 15 over England and four to London. During that time he was awarded the Iron Cross 1st and 2nd Class, Knight's Cross of the House Order of Hohenzollern with Swords and the Hanseatic Cross of Hamburg.

Comparing the number of London raids to those involving an alternative target suggests that von Buttlar's courage was leavened with discretion as the better part of valour. In the first raid on England on 19 January 1915, his *L.6*, with Frgkpt Peter Strasser aboard, suffered a crankshaft failure and after considerable discussion Strasser ordered the airship back to base at Nordholz. Von Buttlar later commanded *L.54* in the 13-airship 'Silent Raid', targeting the British Midlands on 19–20 October 1917. This mission was disastrously undone when gale-force winds scattered the Zeppelins as far as France, resulting in the loss of *L.44*, *L.45*, *L.49*, *L.50* and *L.55*. Von Buttlar, however, identified the impending storm early enough to abandon his plans to hit Sheffield or Manchester, bombing Derby and Nottingham instead. He then guided *L.54* back to Tondern, fighting against winds blowing the airship northward, before alighting with just 205 gallons of fuel left.

During a raid on Grimsby on 12–13 March 1918, *L.54* was struck by anti-aircraft fire, knocking out an engine, but von Buttlar managed to bring the crippled airship home. For this, capping off an extensive combat record, he was awarded the *Orden Pour le Mérite* on 9 April 1918 – the only airship commander so honoured – and given command of the airship base at Tondern. This placed him on the scene to witness the Sopwith Camel raid, launched on 19 July 1918 from the aircraft carrier HMS *Furious*, in which the giant Toska shed was bombed and his *L.54* and *L.60* burned therein, along with a smaller non-rigid airship in the nearby Tobias shed. Cycling to the base, von Buttlar was relieved to learn that his men had removed the bombs from Toska

which, with its open doors, prevented an explosion and limited destruction to the airships. Moreover, just four men were injured, the only fatality of the entire raid being Lt Walter A. Yeulett, whose Camel was lost at sea and whose body subsequently washed ashore in Denmark.

The sole pre-war Zeppelin captain to survive the conflict, von Buttlar continued his career in the much-reduced post-war *Kriegsmarine*, published a memoir, *Zeppeline Gegend England*, in 1931 and subsequently served in the *Luftwaffe*, rising to the rank of *Generalmajor* and being commander of Frankfort airport by the end of World War II.

Married to Ilse Böhm, with whom he had three daughters, von Buttlar spent his last years in Wiesbaden. He died at Berchtesgaden on 3 September 1962.

Horst Treusch von Buttlar-Brandenfels. (Wikimedia Commons/ Public Domain)

WILLIAM LEEFE ROBINSON

From the shock of the first bombs to fall on their soil on 25 December 1914 through to the Zeppelin raids of 1916, Britons seethed with frustration at the German airships which seemed to violate their skies with impunity whilst the army and navy struggled to defend them. Then, on the night of 2–3 September 1916, 2Lt William Leefe Robinson changed that feeling of helplessness during the course of a single action.

Born on 14 July 1895 to Horace Robinson and Elizabeth Eshe Leefe in Kaima Beta estate, India, Robinson was the youngest of seven children. After attending Dragon School, Oxford, the Bishop Cotton School in Bangalore and finally St Bees School, Cumberland, he entered the Royal Military College at Sandhurst on 14 August 1914, obtaining his commission five months later. First posted to the Worcester Regiment, Robinson obtained a transfer to the RFC on 29 March 1915. He then served in No. 4 Sqn at Saint-Omer as a BE 2c observer and as officer in charge of aerial photography until wounded in the right arm by shrapnel on 8 May. After convalescing, Robinson entered pilot training at South Farnborough on 29 June, soloing in a Maurice Farman on 18 July to earn Royal Aero Club Certificate No. 1475. He joined No. 19 Sqn in September and No. 10 Reserve Sqn for Home Defence on 24 December. Soon after, No. 39 (Home Defence) Sqn was formed on 15 April 1916, Robinson being put in charge of its B Flight at Sutton's Farm.

On the night of 25–26 April, Robinson and Capt Arthur Travers Harris fired off a few rounds at *Deutsches Heer* Zeppelin *LZ.97*, which had bombed the village of Fyfield and the parish of Ongar along the River Roding (which Hptm Erich Linnarz had mistaken for the Thames) in Essex, but neither scored a hit. Harris, subsequently a five-victory ace with No. 45 Sqn, would reverse his role in World War II as leader of the Royal Air Force's Bomber Command.

Chagrined at his first airship encounter, Robinson vowed that next time it would be 'either the Zepp or I'. That time came at about 0230hrs on 3 September when he shot Schütte-Lanz airship *SL.11* down in flames near Cuffley. The following day, the RFC's commander, Lt Gen David Henderson, declared, 'I recommend Lt W. L. Robinson for the Victoria Cross, for the most conspicuous gallantry displayed in this successful attack'. Its award to him by King George V on 9 September was one of the swiftest in the medal's history. Robinson also received £4,000 'prize money' from wealthy patriots who had put up bounties for the first airship to be destroyed over England.

On 9 February 1917, Robinson obtained a flight command with No. 48 Sqn, the unit then equipping with a new two-seat fighter in the form of the Bristol F 2A. April found the unit at La Bellevue, France, supporting Gen Robert Nivelle's offensive, and Robinson led six Bristols on No. 48 Sqn's first operational sortie on the 5th. When five Albatros D III fighters attacked, Robinson had his pilots close up, squandering the speed and manoeuvrability that would make the Bristol Fighter a success in the months to come. Over the next ten minutes, his seasoned opponents from *Jagdstaffel* 11 decimated the Bristols – Oblt Manfred *Freiherr* von Richthofen claimed two, Ltn Georg Simon downed another and Vfw Sebastian Festner drove down Robinson's F 2A A3337 near Méricourt. He and his observer, Lt Edward D. Warburton, and the remaining six aircrewmen were taken prisoner – one of von Richthofen's victims, 2Lt Herbert D. K. George, later died of his injuries.

Robinson was held in a succession of prison camps, largely due to his multiple escape attempts. His health had badly deteriorated by the time he was released after the Armistice, and on 31 December 1918 he died in Stanmore, Middlesex, of influenza.

2Lt William Leefe Robinson. (Getty)

While the Home Defence pilots honed their night-flying techniques, a new arsenal of weaponry was being made available to them. New Zealand-born engineer John Pomeroy had developed an explosive bullet that was tested in June 1915 but failed to convince RFC authorities of its practicality. Another explosive 0.303in round, developed by fireworks producer and Royal Navy Volunteer Reserve Wg Cdr Frederick A. Brock, was tested by the RNAS in October and ordered into production in February 1916. In May, the RFC ordered 500,000 of Brock's bullets and three months later acquired a similar number from the persistent Pomeroy. In April 1916, the RFC tested a phosphorus incendiary bullet developed by engineer John F. Buckingham, and in June it accepted a new tracer bullet developed by the makers of the Sparklet soda siphon.

Summer, with its relatively few hours of darkness, brought a lull to Zeppelin activity over England, allowing the RFC to continue organizing its defences. Demands for more men and aeroplanes for the Somme Offensive, starting on 1 July 1916, resulted in the number of Home Defence squadrons being reduced to six, but No. 39 (Home Defence) Sqn, at least, had reached peak strength with 24 aircraft, of which six were new BE 12s – single-seat versions of the BE 2c with a more powerful engine and a single 0.303in Vickers machine gun with interrupter gear. A new airfield at North Weald Bassett in Essex was also put at the disposal of No 39 (Home Defence) Sqn's headquarters flight, which as of 26 July was led by Capt Arthur H. Morton.

At the end of June 1916, the RFC, satisfied with the new incendiary and explosive bullets, dispensed with bombs, although aircraft could still retain a box of Ranken darts. The RNAS kept bombs in its anti-Zeppelin arsenal, however. At that time, the aeroplanes were supplemented by 271 anti-aircraft guns and 258 searchlights.

Home Defence flying in the summer of 1916 was rather more leisurely than that over the Western Front. In the absence of enemy raids, pilots were expected to fly twice a week, just to make sure their aircraft were working. Put in charge of No. 39 (Home Defence) Sqn's B Flight at Sutton's Farm, 2Lt William Leefe Robinson was anything but a hard-nosed disciplinarian. His sister Ruth later described his leadership style:

> He had a remarkable gift for managing men, especially bad characters, and he endeared himself to all who served him. He was never out of temper or depressed, and wherever he was he diffused an air of confidence and hope. He managed to get the best out of everybody and won a general affection because he himself gave out so much of it.

The relatively slow pace notwithstanding, No. 39 (Home Defence) Sqn's steady night-flying practice made a difference. Of 15 aircraft that took off to engage an airship raid on 31 January 1916, 11 crashed and three pilots were killed. Four months later, the squadron reported its airmen taking off and landing without any mishap.

Besides the challenges of flying and navigating at night – which, unlike their German counterparts, they had to do alone – the Home Defence pilots had to put up with the same hardships of freezing temperatures and diminishing oxygen content encountered at high altitudes as their adversaries. That shared experience, once they fully realized it, eventually gave the Home Defence pilots a respect and empathy for the airship crews immeasurably greater than the sentiments held by the general populace on the receiving end of the Zeppelins' depredations.

COMBAT

The first bombs to fall on Britain since January 1915 came from *L.9* on 14–15 April, when Kptltn Heinrich Mathy, on a lone maritime reconnaissance mission west of Terschelling, on the Netherlands coast, took advantage of favourable weather to hit mining villages north of the Tyne near Wallsend, injuring two civilians. Kptltn Strasser led a more serious sortie the next evening when *L.5*, *L.6* and *L.7* departed Nordholz. Kptltn d R Aloys Böcker in *L.5* scattered bombs over Henham Hall, Southwold and Lowestoft in Suffolk, extensively damaging a lumber yard.

Following the Blackwater River, Oblt-z-S Horst Treusch von Buttlar-Brandenfels in *L.6* dropped 24 bombs and incendiary devices, hoping to strike Humberside. They fell instead on Maldon in Essex, where they demolished a workshop and iron shed, damaged a few houses and injured a young girl. 'All of a sudden', declared Mayor Stephen Nunn, 'the war had come to Maldon and was on people's doorsteps'. Ground fire caused leaks in *L.6*'s Nos. 11 and 13 gas cells, but von Buttlar made it home to be promoted to Kapitänleutnant.

Strong headwinds prevented *L.7* from making landfall, and at 0130 hrs Oblt-z-S Werner Peterson gave up. Strasser was aboard *L.7*, and subsequent events seemed to reinforce a growing feeling among Zeppelin crews that, however much they respected their leader, his presence during a raid was a virtual invitation for something to go wrong on the airship in which he flew.

On 29 April, the 'M' class airship *LZ.38*, commanded by Hptm Erich Linnartz, left Brussels-Evère to make the first *Deutsches Heer* Zeppelin raid on England, demolishing six houses in Bury St Edmunds, Orfordness and Aldeburgh in Suffolk. On 10–11 May, he returned to bomb Southend, demolishing Flaxman's timber yard and several shops, killing a woman and injuring two men. The next morning, the British found a small piece of cardboard on Canvey Island bearing an ominous

Flt Sub-Lt Reginald Alexander John Warneford of 1 NAS sits in Morane-Saulnier L 3253, the aeroplane in which he bombed *LZ.37* to destruction on the night of 7 June 1915. (Greg VanWyngarden)

message: 'You English! We have come, and will come again soon – kill or cure – German!'

By the end of May 1915, the *Deutsches Heer* had lost nine airships and the *Kaiserliche Marine* three to various causes on all fronts. By then, too, the Kaiser, bowing to public demand, had sanctioned bombing London east of the Tower. Both services had already been vying to be first to strike at the enemy capital, but on 31 May it was the *Deutsches Heer*'s *LZ.38*, commanded by Linnartz, which passed the coast over Margate and made its way to London, where it dropped a ton of bombs to cause more than £18,000 of damage, kill seven civilians – including three women and a three-year-old girl – and injure 35. On top of that, Sopwith Gunbus 802 of 9 Naval Air Squadron (NAS), returning from patrol, crashed at Hatfield, killing the pilot, Flt Lt Douglas M. Barnes, and injuring his observer, Flt Sub-Lt Benjamin Travers.

On the night of 6–7 June, *LZ.37*, *LZ.38* and *LZ.39* were ordered aloft. *LZ.37*, under the command Oblt Otto von der Haegen, bombed what he identified as Dover, and during the homeward leg dropped more ordnance on Calais. He then headed north-east as searchlights and anti-aircraft guns sought him out, as well as three RNAS squadrons. Coincidentally, on an independent mission, Kptltn Heinrich Mathy navigated *L.9* through the mist to Hull, where he dropped ten explosive and 50 incendiary bombs to cause an unprecedented £44,000 of damage.

Meanwhile, at Saint-Pol-sur-Mer in France, Flt Cdr Arthur M. Longmore, leader of 1 NAS, received a message from the Admiralty reporting three airships returning from a raid. In response he ordered up two Morane-Saulnier L parasols to intercept them and two Farmans to bomb the Zeppelin shed at Brussels-Evère. *LZ.37* was approaching Ostend in Belgium at 0150 hrs on 7 June when it was attacked by Flt Sub-Lt Reginald Alexander John Warneford in Morane-Saulnier L 3253. *LZ.37* rose and its gunners opened fire, Warneford retiring westward as though he had given up, but he then turned about in renewed pursuit.

As *LZ.37* neared Ghent in Belgium at 0215 hrs and began its landing descent, Warneford climbed to 11,000ft. Ten minutes later, he switched off his engine and, gliding above the Zeppelin's hull at 7,000ft, released his bombs in sequence. Just as the sixth one fell, an explosion rent the airship in two, flinging the Morane-Saulnier away, with Warneford struggling to regain control.

'Glowing, smouldering pieces of fabric from the ship's covering fell on my face and neck, and on my comrades', recalled Obersteuermann Alfred Mühler in *LZ.37*'s forward gondola. 'I felt another thunderous crashing and shuddering. The airship had broken up. I lost consciousness'. The next thing Mühler knew, he was in the convent of Saint Elizabeth, where the Zeppelin crashed, killing two nuns and a man. He had been found in the garden along with von der Haegen and other crewmen, all dead or dying. Hospitalized for six weeks for burns and an injured elbow, Mühler was the sole, remarkably lucky, survivor of the first destruction of an airship by an aeroplane.

The Germans' travails were not over. At 0220 hrs, Flt Lt John P. Wilson in Farman 3998 bombed the shed at Brussels-Evère. Ten minutes later, Flt Lt John S. Mills' Farman arrived and came under searchlights and anti-aircraft fire. Climbing to 5,000ft, Mills dropped 12 bombs and saw the shed burning furiously before departing. Destroyed inside was the first Zeppelin to bomb London, *LZ.38*, which had just returned to its 'safe' confines a few hours earlier.

Kptltn Heinrich Mathy's 'lucky' *L.13*, which he navigated with skill and persistence through numerous raids to earn a legendary reputation. Even Capt H. A. Jones in his official air war history proclaimed Mathy 'the greatest airship commander of the war'. (Greg VanWyngarden)

Meanwhile, Warneford had regained control, but his engine was dead, and at 0240 hrs he landed 35 miles behind enemy lines. Bringing his mechanical knowhow into play, he diagnosed and fixed the problem – a broken connection between the gravity and pressure tanks – within 15 minutes. He then restarted his engine and took off just as German cavalry approached. Warneford's fuel gave out at Cap Gris Nez, where he landed on the beach and was briefly 'captured' by French troops.

Once back at Saint-Pol-sur-Mer, Warneford slept for eight hours. On 8 June, he received a telegram from Buckingham Palace:

> I most heartily congratulate you upon your splendid achievement of yesterday in which you single-handedly destroyed an enemy Zeppelin. I have pleasure in conferring upon you the Victoria Cross for this gallant act.
>
> George RI

The RNAS, standing sentinel over the routes to and from Britain, had had a brilliant night, and 'Rex' Warneford was the hero of what proved to be a brief hour. On 17 June, he was made a *Chevalier de la Légion d'Honneur* by the French, then went to Buc, in France, to ferry in a newly delivered Henry Farman F27 with a visiting American journalist, Henry Beech Needham, as passenger. Soon after take-off, however, the aeroplane's supporting booms failed and it crashed, killing both men.

On 20 July, the Kaiser authorized unrestricted bombing of London, provided 'monuments like St Paul's cathedral and the Tower will be spared as far as possible'. On 9 August, Strasser, aboard *L.10*, led five airships over the Channel. Kptltn Udo Loewe in *L.9* evaded three RNAS aeroplanes to drop 42 bombs on Goole in East Yorkshire, which he had mistaken for Hull. No others got that close to their targets. Hit by Dover's 3in naval guns, *L.12* came down in the Channel at 0240 hrs. A torpedo boat towed it to Ostend the next morning, but while being craned onto the pier the airship exploded in flames.

On 7 September, three *Deutsches Heer* airships attacked London, Hptm Richard von Wobeser in *SL.2* causing the most damage with 14 civilians killed and ten injured. Strasser despatched four *Kaiserliche Marine* Zeppelins the following night. Only Mathy's *L.13* reached London, but it wrought the greatest destruction of any one airship during the war, burning out warehouses north of St Paul's that caused £534,387 worth of damage and left 22 dead.

The night of 14–15 October saw *L.11*, *L.14* and *L.15* from Nordholz and *L.13* and *L.16* from Hage, both airfields on the German North Sea coast, strike at the heart of London, although von Buttlar in *L.11* only reached Coltishall, Great Hautbois and Horstead in Norfolk before anti-aircraft fire persuaded him to turn for home after dropping 23 bombs. *L.15*'s Kptltn Joachim Breithaupt ran a gauntlet of flak and searchlights to wreak the most havoc. Overall damage was extensive, and the casualties were the worst of any raid, with 71 people killed and 128 injured. Five aeroplanes rose against the airships and 18-year-old Lt John Slessor tried to attack *L.15* with Ranken darts, only to see the Zeppelin turn its nose up and climb, leaving his BE 2c hopelessly behind.

There would be no more raids in 1915, but the 21 that had come that year killed 208 civilians and injured 432. By and large the English reaction was less one of fear than of anger – anger at the Germans for indiscriminately striking at civilian targets, and at their home forces for not doing more to stop them. Almost a year would pass before that state of affairs changed significantly.

1916 – THE BOGEY IS LAID

Strasser started 1916 leading a nine-airship raid on 31 January, causing moderate damage. Von Buttlar's *L.11* – with Stasser aboard – was handicapped by two tons of ice and rain, leaving it unable to reach 6,700ft, and blinded by fog until Strasser aborted the mission. *L.19* strayed over The Netherlands, whose anti-aircraft fire brought it down in the North Sea. The airship was quickly spotted by the British trawler *King Stephen*, which was fishing in prohibited waters with only eight men on board. Consequently, its captain left, hoping to direct a naval vessel to the Germans' rescue. By the time he arrived at Grimsby to report the incident, however, it was too late for *L.19*'s 16-man crew. Eight of the 20 aircraft that rose against the airships that night crashed and two pilots died of injuries.

Seven *Kaiserliche Marine* and three *Deutsches Heer* Zeppelins attacked on 31 March. *L.15*, hit by anti-aircraft fire from the Dartford battery and attacked by BE 2cs flown by 2Lts Claude A. Ridley and Albert de B. Brandon, went down off the coast, where 16 of its 17 crewmen were rescued by the British armed trawler HMS *Olivine* and transferred to the destroyer HMS *Vulture*. Fifteen more raids between 2 April and 25 August added widely varying amounts to England's woes and continuing frustration to the RFC's airmen.

A re-touched photograph from the *London Illustrated News* shows the remains of *L.15* – all but one of whose 18-man crew survived to be evacuated – on 2 April 1916. Although 2Lts Claude A. Ridley and Alfred Brandon attacked *L.15*, for which Ridley received the Military Medal and Brandon the Military Cross, the main agent of its downfall was probably the anti-aircraft battery at Dartford. (Greg VanWyngarden)

Then, on 2 September, 12 *Kaiserliche Marine* and four *Deutsches Heer* airships left their North Sea bases for England. At 2305 hrs, the telephone rang at No. 39 (Home Defence) Sqn's aerodrome at Sutton's Farm and the orderly relayed the message – 'Take air raid action!' 2Lt William Leefe Robinson, in BE 2c 2693, took off to patrol between Sutton's Farm and Joyce Green. At about 0115 hrs on 3 September, he and two other No. 39 (Home Defence) Sqn pilots attacked *LZ.98* as it returned from bombing Tilbury, but the airship escaped unscathed.

Meanwhile, at 0100 hrs, Schütte-Lanz airship *SL.11* reached the outskirts of London. As its last bombs fell, three BE 2cs of No. 39 (Home Defence) Sqn, flown by 2Lts J. I. Mackay, B. H. Hunt and Robinson, who saw it in the searchlights, dived at the airship from the south-east. *SL.11* eluded the searchlights and the BEs in a cloud bank, but Robinson saw it re-emerge and dived to rake its underside with a drum of Lewis fire. This seemed to have no effect, nor did a second pass along the airship's flank. Placing a third magazine in his weapon, Robinson approached behind and below the elevators and rudder, focusing his gunfire on a single area. This produced a pink glow within the airship, which subsequently burst into 100ft-high flames before crashing in a beet field near Cuffley, killing Hptm Wilhelm Schramm and his 15 crewmen. Its fiery descent was visible for 60 miles, and London erupted in joyful pandemonium.

Robinson was awarded the Victoria Cross and his feat seemed to set a definite precedent, for it was followed by a rapid succession of further intercepts. During an attack on London on 24 September, *L.33* was riddled by anti-aircraft fire, attacked by 2Lt Brandon and finally brought down near Colchester in Essex, where its crew surrendered. On that same night, 2Lt Frederick Sowrey of No. 39 (Home Defence) Sqn destroyed *L.32*, killing its entire crew. On 2 October, yet another No. 39 (Home Defence) Sqn member, 2Lt Wulstan J. Tempest, sent *L.31* blazing to earth near Potters Bar, Hertfordshire, its captain, the enterprising and hitherto lucky Heinrich Mathy, leaping to his death rather than being burnt alive like his 18 crewmen.

Other units also got into the act. On 27 November, 2Lt Ian V. Pyott of No. 36 (Home Defence) Sqn, in BE 2c 2738, destroyed *L.34*, killing Kptltn d R Max Dietrich and 19 crewmen. Later that night, three RNAS pilots from Great Yarmouth – Flt Lt Egbert Cadbury and Flt Sub-Lts Gerard W. R. Fane and Edward L. Pulling – shared credit for burning *L.21*, which fell into the sea nine miles east of Lowestoft, killing Oblt-z-S Kurt Frankenburg and his 16 men.

While 2Lt William Leefe Robinson poses in his BE 2c 2693, two mechanics show the damage done to the upper-wing centre section by the pilot's own machine gun on the night of 3 September 1916. (Philip Jarrett Collection)

A close up of the cockpit and armament fitted to 2Lt William Leefe Robinson's BE 2c 2693, this photograph being taken at Eastchurch on 6 June 1916 prior to the aircraft joining B Flight of No. 39 (Home Defence) Sqn at Sutton's Farm. The Strange mount for its upward-firing Lewis gun is clearly visible. (Greg VanWyngarden)

A New Zealander who got his law degree in 1906, 2Lt Alfred de Bathe Brandon travelled to England, joined the RFC and qualified as a pilot in December 1915. He went on to have more than one encounter with Zeppelins, getting at least partial credit in the demise of two. (The David Marks Collection)

L.31 overflies the battleship Ostfriesland in 1916. The 'R' class airship would meet its end on 2 October of that year at the hands of 2Lt Wulstan J. Tempest of No. 39 (Home Defence) Sqn. Kaptltn Heinrich Mathy, for whom '13' had been a lucky number but '31' the opposite, leapt to his death rather than burn aboard the airship. (Christophe Cony)

In a total of 23 airship raids in 1916, the Germans had dropped 125 tons of bombs, killing 293 people and injuring 691. Although these figures reflect the fact that the airships had inflicted more carnage on England's civil population than during the previous year, the vital factor of the campaign's effect on morale underwent a sea change. In 1915, the only air-to-air success against a Zeppelin had been by the RNAS on the far side of the Channel. In the last third of 1916, no fewer than six airships were shot down over England or near the coast, where their demise could be locally observed. The British public could look forward to still more terror from the sky, but the high-flying giants were no longer meting it out with impunity. The bogey had been laid.

1917 – HIGH HOPES AND SILENT RAIDERS

Soon after SL.11's demise, the *Deutsches Heer* abandoned airship raids in favour of aeroplanes, and only Strasser's pleas kept the *Kaiserliche Marine* from following suit. Besides their overall nuisance value, he argued that the Zeppelins would still be useful

British troops secure and examine the remains of *L.33* (*LZ.76*) after it came down in Little Wigborough on 24 September 1916. (Getty)

harassing industrial targets in the Midlands and northern England, where the *Luftstreitskräfte*'s Gothas and Staaken *Riesenflugzeuge* could not reach. Still, the airships were undeniably vulnerable to aeroplanes, and the German Admiralty hoped that the new, more streamlined designs would offer increased speed sufficient to avoid interception. On 17 January 1917, however, Strasser advocated another route – increasing their operational ceiling. The first product of that proposal, *L.42*, rose to 19,700ft during its inaugural flight on 10 March.

Although his aircrews paid a high ergonomic price for operating at such altitudes, Strasser optimistically pressed for production of the new 'Height Climbers', and on 16 March *L.42* joined *L.35*, *L.39*, *L.40* and *L.41*, all modified to reach higher altitudes, in a debut over London that never came off. Unexpected storms blew the airships off course, on top of which *L.42*, with Strasser aboard, suffered an engine breakdown and was fortunate to make it to Jüterbog with only an hour's fuel remaining.

On 14 May, *L.23* and *L.22* took off on a reconnaissance mission. The latter's wireless message upon take-off, revealing its regular patrol route off Terschelling, was intercepted by the British. Thus notified, at 0330 hrs the RNAS base at Great Yarmouth despatched Curtiss H-12B Large America flying boat 8666 – crewed by Flt Sub-Lt Robert Leckie, Flt Lt Christopher J. Galpin, CPO V. F. Whatling and Air Mechanic O. R. Laycock – to intercept. At 0445 hrs, Galpin spotted an airship, and as Leckie took over the controls, he manned the twin forward Lewis machine guns. Leckie closed to 50 yards and Galpin fired a mix of Brock, Buckingham and Pomeroy rounds into *L.22*'s starboard quarter until both guns jammed. Galpin reported that, 'As we began to turn I thought I saw a slight glow inside the envelope, and 15 seconds later, when she came in sight on our other side, she was hanging tail down at an angle of 45 degrees, with the lower half of her envelope thoroughly alight'. Kptltn Ulrich Lehmann and his 20 crewmen all died.

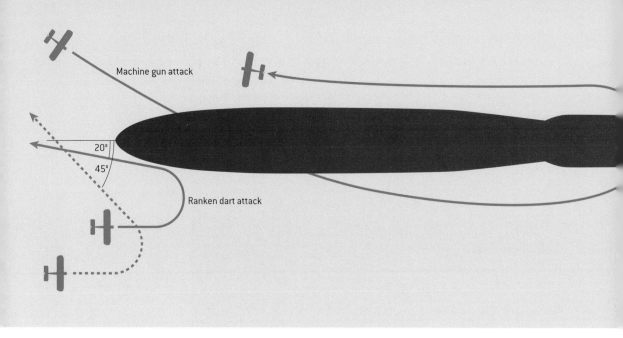

Machine gun attack

20°
45°

Ranken dart attack

British nightfighters seldom invited midair mishaps by operating too near to one another when engaging a Zeppelin. Upon contact with the enemy, the fighter would approach head-on, then turn about and fly 150–750ft above the Zeppelin's bow at a 20–45-degree approach angle to drop its Hales bombs or Ranken darts. A similar approach was taken with Lewis guns on the Strange mount, but usually attacking from underneath.

Six Zeppelins made for London on 23 May, but *L.44* – again, by dubious coincidence, with Strasser along – suffered three breakdowns and limped back to Nordholz on two engines. Kptltn Hermann Kraushaar claimed that *L.43* reached the capital, but his 38 bombs only damaged several cottages, killing one man. Fog and thunderstorms limited further damage to £599 worth in Norwich by *L.40* and *L.45*.

On 13 June, *L.46* and *L.48* patrolled the U-boat routes while other Zeppelins covered a minesweeping operation 40 miles north of Terschelling. At 0536 hrs, *L.43* reported its arrival over the Terschelling Bank lightship, but Felixstowe had already despatched another H-12B, 8677 crewed by Flt Lt Basil D. Hobbs, Flt Sub-Lt Robert F. L. Dickey, wireless operator H. M. Davies and engineer A. W. Goody, at 0515 hrs. At 0840 hrs, Hobbs was near Vlieland at 500ft when he spotted an airship 1,000ft above him, heading due north, and climbed to attack.

'As we approached the Zeppelin we dived for her tail at about 100 knots', Hobbs reported. 'Her number *L43* was observed on the tail and bow, also the Maltese cross in a black circle. Midship gun opened fire with tracer ammunition and when about 100[ft] above Sub-Lieut. Dickie [sic] opened fire with Brock and Pomeroy ammunition as the machine passed diagonally over the tail from starboard to port. After two bursts the Zeppelin burst into flames'.

Kraushaar and his 23 crewmen perished with the first 'Height Climber' to fall, ironically at low altitude. In consequence, airships were ordered to conduct their reconnaissance flights at no lower than 13,000ft, although it was virtually impossible to spot submerged U-boats or mines from that height.

Many German crewmen regarded the 'Height Climbers'' next sortie to London, on 16 June, as a suicide mission, since the summer solstice was but a week away, affording only three hours of semi-darkness. Strong crosswinds kept *L.46* and *L.47* in their sheds, whilst *L.44* and *L.45* returned with engine trouble. Kept from London by high winds and a thunderstorm, *L.42* bombed Ramsgate in Kent, where one 660lb bomb struck a naval ammunition depot and all but destroyed the naval base, with £28,159 worth of damage. It also killed three civilians and injured a further 14 and two servicemen. In spite of six aircraft seeking it out, *L.42* returned to Nordholz after 39 hours, but Dietrich's radioed report to Strasser was more grim than triumphant due to what he spotted 70 miles away: 'At 3.35, two points abaft the port beam, a red ball of fire suddenly appeared, which quickly grew bigger and in falling, showed the shape of a Zeppelin airship'.

Hampered by a frozen compass and a malfunctioning starboard engine, *L.48*, commanded by Kptltn d R Franz Georg Eichler and with the deputy commander of airships, Kvtkpt Victor Schütze, aboard, tried to target Harwich in Essex, but its 13 bombs fell on a field at Kirton, five miles to the north. As the airship turned for home at 17,000ft, three aircraft that had been struggling up attacked it simultaneously at 0325 hrs on 17 June. These were 2Lt Loudon P. Watkins in BE 12 6610 of No. 37 (Home Defence) Squadron, based at Goldhanger, Essex, and two aircraft from the RFC's Experimental Station at Ordfordness in Suffolk – DH 2 A5058, flown by Capt Robert H. M. S. Saundby, and FE 2b B401, crewed by 2Lt Frank D. Holder and Sgt Sydney Ashby. Their combined gunfire set the front and rear gas cells of *L.48* ablaze, and it fell stern-first near Theberton, Suffolk. Of its 18-man crew, only Ltn-z-S Otto Meith and Machinist's Mates Wilhelm Uecker and Heinrich Ellerkamm survived, saved by the Zeppelin's collapsing Duralumin structure as it crashed to earth. Uecker, however, would eventually succumb to his internal injuries on Armistice Day.

Saundby, Holder and Watkins received the Military Cross and Ashby the Military Medal for their role in *L.48*'s destruction – on top of which Saundby, a former DH 2 pilot in No. 24 Sqn in 1916, could claim his ace-making fifth victory. Much of *L.48*'s

A BE 12b with flame shrouds over its exhausts. This single-seat nightfighter development of the BE 2c was meant to be powered by the 200hp Hispano-Suiza 8B, but Daimler built only 150 because of the greater need for SE 5as using those engines. A BE 12, powered by a 150hp RAF 4a engine, shared in the type's only Home Defence success when it took part in shooting down *L.48* on 17 June 1917. (Greg VanWyngarden)

The Germans had high hopes for their new 'Height Climber' Zeppelins, but the fate of *L.48* on 17 June 1917 showed how forlorn those hopes were. (Greg VanWyngarden)

burnt framework, its control car and a Maybach engine remained to provide British Intelligence with its first details of the 'Height Climbers', which thus far had not fared auspiciously.

Worse was to come. On 21 August, *L.23* was reconnoitring over the 3rd Light Cruiser Squadron 30 miles west of Bovberg, on the Jutland coast, when it was unexpectedly attacked by Sopwith Pup N6430, in which Flt Sub-Lt Bernard A. Smart had risen from a 'flying off platform' atop the forward gun turret of the cruiser HMS *Yarmouth*. The Pup pilot subsequently recalled his engagement with the airship as follows:

I could see a man and an object unpleasantly like a machine gun on top of the envelope, and I now realized the time had come. I was now at 7,000ft and the Zeppelin a thousand feet below at an angle of 45 degrees, and I was still heading straight for her stern. I pushed forward the control stick and dived. The speed indicator went with a rush up to 150mph and I rammed down the machine gun's operating lever, and held it there. The gun spat out and the Zeppelin was soon a mass of flames and had dropped so that the nose was pointing to the sky at an angle of 45 degrees while the flames were fast licking up towards the nose. An object was adrift from the forward end of the Zeppelin, which I first took to be some part of the fabric falling off, but on looking again I discovered it to be a man descending in a parachute. He was the only one, and as he floated down, he and I seemed to be alone in space. I turned until my compass was in the opposite direction to that when I had been chasing the Zeppelin and then looked back to have a last glance at the blaze. The wreck had just reached the sea, only the very tip of it still being intact.

The Germans attributed the mystifying loss of *L.23* with Oblt-z-S Bernhard Dinter and 17 crewmen to shipboard gunfire and the British saw fit to keep them in the dark, awarding Smart the Distinguished Service Order (DSO) for 'a specially brilliant feat' and withholding further details as late as 1919. Smart, who also got the *Croix de Guerre*, subsequently flew a Sopwith Camel off HMS *Furious* to bomb the Zeppelin sheds at Tondern on 19 July 1918, adding a bar to his DSO.

Zeppelin raids aimed at the Midlands on 21 August and 24 September achieved little, save for two crashes and three airmen killed among the 37 aeroplanes that tried to intercept them. Then on 19 October orders reached Ahlhorn, Nordholz, Tondern and Mittmundhafen for 13 Zeppelins to 'Attack Middle England, industrial region of Sheffield, Manchester, Liverpool, etc.' Eleven crossed the Channel at such heights that the British could not even hear their engines. Searchlights proved of little use, London's guns went unfired rather than betray their position and none of the 73 aeroplanes that took off reached the airships. However, gale-force winds encountered at altitude that night scattered most participants in the so-called 'Silent Raid' south and east as far as the Vosges region of France. One exception was von Buttlar in *L.54*, who recognized the signs of impending disaster and settled for bombing Derby and Nottingham, prior to retiring to Tondern.

Five were less fortunate. Climbing to escape French fighters, *L.55* reached a record altitude of 24,600ft on the return flight, but was wrecked while force-landing at Tiefenort in Germany. *L.45* made it to Northampton and London, where its scattered bombs killed 24 people and injured nine. However, it was then attacked south of the Medway by Lt Thomas B. Pritchard in a BE 2c of No. 39 (Home Defence) Sqn, before high winds blew the Zeppelin southward and engine failure forced it down at Sisteron in France, where Kptltn Waldemar Kölle and his crew burned the remains. The crewmen subsequently boasted to their French captors that they had flown from Denmark via London and Paris to the French Riviera in less than 24 hours. Hit at 0645 hrs by anti-aircraft fire at almost 4,000ft over Saint-Clément in central France, *L.44* burned with all 18 of its crew.

Over the Vosges mountains near France's eastern border with Germany, two errant Zeppelins came under attack by French Nieuports. Kptnltn Hans Geyer's *L.49* was

A French illustration shows its famed 75mm field gun, adapted for an anti-aircraft role, in action against German airships. On the night of 19–20 October, the French guns scored when *L.44* drifted over Saint-Clément, near Lunéville, and was shot down in flames by the *174ème section special de canons speciaux (Défense Contre Avions)*, along with its 18-man crew. (Greg VanWyngarden)

pursued by Lt Charles Lefèvre, Sous-Lt Charles Lafargue, MdL Gontran de la Marque and Cpls Marcel Denis, Philippe Gresset and René Vandendorpe of *escadrille* N152, who shared the credit for bringing it down intact near Bourbonne-les-Bains. Cpl Denis also traded fire with *L.50*'s gunners before low fuel forced him to land at Rouvres-la-Chétive in eastern France. The airship was drifting along at 6,500ft when Sous-Lt Henri Léon Hirsch and Cpl Alfred Ambrosio of N151 attacked it, killing several crewmen. At that point, with three engines out, Kptltn Roderich Schwonder deliberately drove it into a hillside near Dammartin. The control gondola broke off and 16 crewmen who had leapt clear before impact were taken prisoner. Thus lightened, the airship lifted off again and, carried by the wind, was last seen near Fréjus in south-eastern France before it and the four remaining crewmen aboard vanished somewhere over the Mediterranean Sea.

1918 – LAST NAILS IN A FLYING COFFIN

Still determined to prove the Zeppelin's worth, Strasser, aboard *L.62*, led an attack on the Midlands on 12 March 1918, doing £3,474 worth of damage and killing a civilian. He aborted a raid the following night due to veering westerly winds, but Martin Dietrich, already over Northumberland in *L.42*, pressed on to West Hartlepool and dropped 21 bombs, causing £14,280 worth of damage, killing eight civilians and injuring 29, then eluded two FEs from No. 36 (Home Defence) Sqn to make it home. During another raid on the Midlands on 12 April, only two

Sopwith 2F1 'Ships Camels' assemble on the forward deck of the aircraft carrier HMS *Furious* prior to being despatched on a historic pre-emptive strike against the Zeppelin sheds at Tondern on 19 July 1918. (Getty)

of five Zeppelins made landfall. *L.61* dropped 15 bombs on Wigan in Greater Manchester, causing £11,673 worth of damage, killing seven people and wounding 12.

On 19 July, the Royal Navy launched another of its innovative pre-emptive strikes. Six Sopwith 2F1 'Ships Camels' took off from the carrier *Furious* to bomb Tondern, destroying *L.54* and *L.60* in their shed.

Meanwhile, on 8 July, a new flagship for the *Marine-Luftschiff-Abteilung*, the 'X' class *L.70* with seven engines and a 20mm Becker cannon in its arsenal, emerged from Factory Shed II at Friedrichshafen, and its designated captain, Kptltn Johann von Lossnitzer, flew it to Nordholz. On 1 August, it and two other Zeppelins reconnoitred the Dogger Bank, dropping some bombs on Commodore Reginald Y. Tyrwhitt's Harwich Light Cruiser Force. Although none of his ships were hit, a surprised Tyrwhitt commented that the airship commanders 'were losing their sense of caution, and that it would be worthwhile, next time, to take a fighting aeroplane'.

L.70's next target would be England. On 5 August, Strasser ordered *L.63* from Ahlhorn, *L.56* from Wittmundhafen and *L.53* and *L.65* from Nordholz to rendezvous for yet another sally, with him joining the relatively new and inexperienced von Lossnitzer aboard *L.70*. Weather conditions – 75 degrees Fahrenheit, 85 per cent humidity and an unprecedented low barometric reading of 29.77 – handicapped the raiders' ascent, while steadily decreasing west winds resulted in their advancing to 60 nautical miles from the coast at 1830 hrs while there was still daylight. By then they had struggled to 17,000ft, but Strasser compounded the danger by sending last orders to his captains by wireless at 2100 hrs. At that time, the Leman Tail lightship, moored 30 miles off the Norfolk coast, spotted three airships ten miles to the north, moving west-north-west in 'V' formation.

Britain was having a bank holiday weekend and Great Yarmouth was hosting a 'Grand Fete' sponsored by the Royal Navy in aid of the Missions to Seamen when air raid warnings came in just after 2100 hrs. Within 35 minutes, 15 aircraft were either

Flt Lt Egbert Cadbury was flying a BE 2c with the RNAS when he shared in the destruction of L.21 on 28 November 1916, and went on to team up with Maj Robert Leckie in an RAF DH 4 to confront the last Zeppelin raid on Britain on 5 August 1918. (Topfoto)

airborne or taking off. Among the first up was Egbert Cadbury, now an RAF major and commander of No. 212 Sqn (Land Flight), who outraced Capt C. B. Sproatt into the cockpit of Airco DH 4 A8032, while Maj Robert Leckie, CO of No. 228 Sqn (Boat Flight), clambered into the observer's position behind him. Two 110lb bombs were still under the wings as Cadbury hastened skyward at 2105 hrs.

Sighting the Zeppelins against the fading twilight, Cadbury pulled his bomb release and climbed to 16,400ft. At 2220 hrs, he approached the leading airship head-on and slightly to port so as to 'avoid any hanging obstructions'. Leckie's single Lewis gun lacked sights and his first rounds missed. He could see his fiery Pomeroy ZPT rounds streaking away, however, and used them to correct his aim. 'The ZPT was seen to blow a great hole in the fabric and a fire started which quickly ran along the entire length of [the] Zeppelin', Leckie reported. 'The Zeppelin raised her bows as if in an effort to escape, then plunged seaward, a blazing mass. The airship was completely consumed in about three-quarters of a minute'.

Horrified, Kvtkpt der R Edward Prölls of *L.53* and Kptltn Walter Dose of *L.65* turned east and dumped their water ballast. As they rose, Cadbury made for *L.65* and Leckie fired at it, only to suffer a double feed jam which his hands – in -60 degree temperatures at that altitude – were too frozen to rectify. Cadbury raised the DH 4's nose to bring his twin Vickers into play, but he was at maximum altitude and his aeroplane stalled. By then DH 9 D5802, crewed by Capt Douglas B. G. Jardine and Lt Edward R. Munday, had arrived and put some 340 rounds through *L.65*'s rear gas cell before it climbed away. After a difficult 16 hrs 20 min flight, Dose brought his airship back to base for repairs. The other three Zeppelins likewise returned, having landed no bombs on any English target.

Returning through 12,000ft of cloud at night, 'Bertie' Cadbury had a terrifying half hour until he spotted rows of lights pointing inland from Hunstanton, on the north Norfolk coast, and landed safely at nearby Sedgeford. 'To my horror I discovered that my bombs had failed to release', he added, 'and that I had landed in a machine which I thought was certain to crash and catch fire with two 110lb bombs on board. Also, that my life-saving belt had been eaten through by acid from an accumulator'. Both he and Leckie were gazetted for the Distinguished Flying Cross on 21 August.

Jardine and Munday were less fortunate, crashing in the sea, as did Lt George F. Hodson in one of three 2F1 Camels that had scrambled up from Burgh Castle, also in Norfolk – all of them drowned. Additionally, Lt Frank A. Benitz of No. 33 (Home Defence) Sqn, taking off from Scampton in Bristol F 2B C4698, crash-landed at Atwick aerodrome on the East Yorkshire coast. His observer, 2Lt H. Lloyd-Williams, was badly hurt, and Benitz died of his injuries the next day.

L.70 came down five miles north-west of the Blakeney Overfalls' bell buoy, along with Frgkpt Peter Strasser, von Lossnitzer and 20 crewmen. Dying with Strasser was the *Kaiserliche Marine*'s airship campaign against Britain.

In retrospect, Cadbury was glad that *L.53* and *L.65* got away, regarding their destruction as unnecessary overkill. As Leckie put it, 'We accomplished our object in that the shooting down of *L.70* put an end to the Zeppelin raiding of England'. *L.53* was not destined to survive for long, however. During a reconnaissance sortie on 11 August, it encountered a 2F1 Camel that had taken off from a lighter towed by the destroyer HMS *Redoubt* – an arrangement developed by Cdr Charles Rumney Samson to provide Commodore Tyrwhitt with the air defence he had requested earlier that month. Flown by Lt Stuart Douglas Culley, Camel N6812 rose to 19,000ft and destroyed *L.53* near Terschelling, killing Prölls and his 20 crewmen. Ditching near the lighter, Culley was recovered along with his Camel, which is now preserved in the Imperial War Museum in London.

L.53's demise put paid at last to the Zeppelin as a serious instrument of war. Although Kvtkpt Paul Werther was appointed Leader of Airships, the *Kaiserliche Marine* was relying more on floatplanes for reconnaissance, with Claude Dornier's giant, long-range RS III and RS IV flying boats offering greater promise for the future. Shortages in materials and personnel led to flight restrictions and the dismantling of airship sheds.

The *Marine-Luftschiff-Abteilung* was effectively grounded until the Armistice on 11 November 1918, which stipulated the confiscation of ships and airships alike by the Inter-Allied Commission. On 23 June 1919, two days after the mass scuttling of the surrendered German battle fleet off Scapa Flow, von Buttlar and other naval 'loyalists' wrecked *L.14*, *L.41*, *L.42*, *L.63* and *L.65* at Nordholz, while *L.52* and *L.56* were similarly sabotaged at Wittmundhafen. Other Zeppelins were seized by the Allies and the factory at Friedrichshafen was demolished.

OVERLEAF

On 5 August 1918, Frgkpt Peter Strasser boarded the new 'X' class *L.70*, commanded by Kptltn Johann von Lossnitzer, to lead *L.63*, *L.56*, *L.53* and *L.65* on another raid against England. Weather conditions handicapped their progress, and at 2100 hrs the Leman Tail lightship spotted three airships off the Norfolk coast. Among the first of 15 British aircraft that took off to intercept was DH 4 A8032, flown by Maj Egbert Cadbury, commander of No. 212 Sqn (Land Flight), with Maj Robert Leckie, CO of No. 228 Sqn (Boat Flight) in the observer's pit. By 2220 hrs, Cadbury was at 16,400ft, approaching the leading airship head-on and slightly to port so as to 'avoid any hanging obstructions'. Leckie's single Lewis gun lacked sights and his first rounds missed, but the fiery Pomeroy ZPT ammunition allowed him to correct his aim. 'The ZPT was seen to blow a great hole in the fabric and a fire started which quickly ran along the entire length of [the] Zeppelin', Leckie reported. Cadbury then made for *L.65*, but Leckie's Lewis suffered a double feed jam, and when the pilot raised the DH 4's nose to bring his twin Vickers into play the aeroplane stalled. Cadbury subsequently landed safely at Sedgeford. *L.70* crashed five miles north-west of the Blakeney Overfalls bell buoy, killing von Lossnitzer, his 20 crewmen and Peter Strasser.

Jim Laurier

A 2F1 Camel – possibly N6812 – and a handful of sailors get a thorough soaking on lighter *H3* while being towed behind an unidentified naval vessel at high-speed in the summer of 1918. The aircraft lacks covers and weapons, the lighter is close to land and the handling party hardly seemed primed for action, all of which suggests that this photograph was taken during trials. On 11 August 1918, Lt Stuart Douglas Culley took off from the lighter *H5* in N6812 and climbed to 19,000ft to attack, and destroy, *L.53* near Terschelling. The airship had been carrying out a reconnaissance mission over Royal Navy vessels at the time. (IWM Q 65606)

SELECTED INDIVIDUAL ZEPPELIN HISTORIES

LZ.74 (L.32)

Launched on 4 August 1916, it made three attacks on England, dropping a total of 15,120lb of bombs. Commanded by Kptltn Werner Peterson, it took part in the night raid of 23/24 September 1916 with *LZ.72*, *LZ.76* and *LZ.78*. The airship was intercepted and destroyed by 2Lt Frederick Sowrey of No. 39 (Home Defence) Sqn in an RAF BE 2c on 24 September near Great Burstead, Essex, all the crew perishing. Their bodies were originally buried at Great Burstead, then, in 1966, they were exhumed and reburied at Cannock Chase German Military Cemetary in Staffordshire.

LZ.76 (L.33)

Launched on 30 August 1916, *LZ.76* was also part of the Zeppelin group that bombed London and surrounding counties on the night of 23/24 September 1916. During its first mission, in which 7,055lb of bombs had been dropped, the airship was seriously damaged by an anti-aircraft shell. Its commander, Kptltn Alois Böcker, changed course over Essex and was attacked by No. 39 (Home Defence) Sqn nightfighters from Hainault Farm and hit several times – credit for disabling *LZ.76* was given to BE 2c 4544 flown by 2Lt Alfred de Bathe Brandon. Even after dropping guns and equipment, Böcker decided he could not make it back across the North Sea, force-landing in Little Wigborough, Essex, on 24 September with no fatalities. The crew was only partly successful in burning the hull, and British engineers examined the skeleton and later used the plans drawn up from this examination as a basis for the construction of the R33-class airships post-war.

LZ.61 (L.21)

Launched on 10 January 1916, *LZ.61* completed 17 reconnaissance missions and ten attacks on England, dropping a total of 31,839lb of bombs. It was eventually intercepted and destroyed on 28 November 1916 by Flt Lt Egbert Cadbury, flying BE 2c 8265, Flt Sub-Lt Gerard William Reginald Fane, flying BE 2c 8421, and Flt Sub-Lt Edward Laston Pulling, flying BE 2c 8626, with phosphorous rounds. *L.21* fell into the sea about eight miles east of Lowestoft. There were no survivors.

LZ.78 (L.34)

Launched on 22 September 1916, this airship undertook three reconnaissance missions and two attacks on England, dropping a total of 8,580lb of bombs. It took part in the raid on the night of 23–24 September 1916. *LZ.78* was intercepted and destroyed by 2Lt Ian Pyott in BE 2c 2738 off Hartlepool on 27 November 1916.

LZ.72 (L.31)

Launched on 12 July 1916, this airship made six attacks on England, dropping a total of 42,794lb of bombs. It also completed an important reconnaissance mission in fleet operations against Sunderland. Participating in the Zeppelin raid of 23/24 September 1916, *LZ.72* was intercepted and destroyed by 2Lt W. J. Tempest on 2 October 1916 near Potters Bar, north of London. Its commander on this fateful mission was veteran Kptltn Heinrich Mathy, who died along with his crew after he jumped from the flaming Zeppelin. The crew was originally buried at Potters Bar, but later exhumed and reburied at Cannock Chase.

SL.11

Launched on 1 August 1916, *SL 11* was built by Luftschiffbau Schütte-Lanz and thus was not classed as a Zeppelin. Based at Spich and commanded by Hptm Wilhelm Schramm, the airship bombed St Albans in Hertfordshire in the early hours of 3 September 1916. It was then attacked by 2Lt William Leefe Robinson in a BE 2c, who brought it down with incendiary ammunition at Cuffley. The crew was killed, being buried at Potters Bar Cemetery before being re-interred at Cannock Chase in 1962. Robinson was awarded the Victoria Cross for the destruction of *SL.11*.

STATISTICS AND ANALYSIS

In hard numbers, German airships made 51 raids on England to drop just over 192 tons of bombs, resulting in the deaths of 557 people and 1,358 injured. Material damage amounted to £1,527,585 – roughly the price of nine late-model 'Height Climber' Zeppelins. To that one might add the collateral damage done to the Home Defence aircraft in the course of their duties. Although there is no evidence of a confirmed loss to airship gunners, the hazards of nocturnal flying resulted in at least nine crashes upon landing, resulting in seven deaths and three injuries. In addition, on the night of 9–10 August 1915, Flt Lt D. K. Johnston of 2 Wing RNAS was killed when his Farman was shot down during an attempt to bomb the newly returned *L.12* in its shed at Ostend.

The cost to the Germans was much higher – 19 airships and most of their crews shot down and another 11 destroyed in accidents during the campaign. For comparison, German aeroplanes made 27 raids and dropped 2,772 bombs totalling 246,774lb on British targets, killing 857 people and injuring 2,058, but causing slightly less damage at £1,418,272. Total losses came to 62 Gothas and *Riesenflugzeuge*. The overall conclusion is that not only did the rapid advance of aeroplane development on the part of the British defenders overtake the Zeppelin, but so did the development of German aeroplanes into bombers which, while dropping less bomb tonnage, caused more loss of life and almost as much destruction.

That said, it seems ironic in retrospect that the last Zeppelin raid on Britain occurred months after the last aeroplane raid. On 19 May 1918, 38 Gothas of *Kampfgeschwader der Obersten Heeresleitung* 3 and three Giants of *Riesenfleuzeugabtelung* 501 attacked

The Star announces the latest two Zeppelins, *L.34* and *L.21*, 'Destroyed on East Coast' on 28 November 1916. This success saw the morale of the British public at year-end in a state much changed from 1915, and left Peter Strasser concerned over the future of his beloved airships. (Greg VanWyngarden)

London, only to encounter a massive and by then well-practiced defence from the searchlights, anti-aircraft guns and nightfighters. The raid caused £117,317 worth of damage, killed 49 people and injured 177, but six Gothas were shot down and a seventh forced to land after a long pursuit by Lts Edward E. Turner and Henry B. Barwise of No. 141 Sqn – the first aerial victory tallied at their aerodrome at Biggin Hill in Kent.

After a year-and-a-half of frustration, No. 39 (Home Defence) Sqn's BE 2cs produced a sudden succession of successes, making household names of (from left) 2Lts 'Billy' Leefe Robinson, Wulstan Tempest and Fred Sowrey. (Getty)

One of the new 'X' class Zeppelins, *L.71* was among the three that Strasser had in mind for a transatlantic bombing raid on New York until Adm Reinhard Scheer rejected his proposal on 19 July 1918. (Greg VanWyngarden)

That did it for the Gothas. The German High Command conceived a '*Feuerplan*' involving mass aerial attacks with incendiary bombs on London and Paris to be launched in September 1918, but the scheme was never carried out, probably due to concerns regarding Allied reprisals.

Ignoring all such setbacks and misgivings, Frgkpt Peter Strasser never gave up on his increasingly forlorn hope that Zeppelins constituted a viable strategic weapon to counter the Allies' growing strength, to which the United States was adding its own preponderance.

On 27 November 1916, 2Lt Ian V. Pyott of No. 36 (Home Defence) Sqn, in BE 2c 2738, destroyed *L.34* off Hartlepool. (Steve Suddaby)

In fact, with *L.70* operational and two sisters nearing completion, he approached Adm Reinhard Scheer on 18 July with a plan to despatch the three 'Super Zeppelins' with reduced bomb loads and increased fuel on a transatlantic flight to bomb the port facilities in New York. Scheer wearily consented to read Strasser's proposal, but returned it the next day, probably without reading it through, with a terse pencilled response, '*R.S., nein*'.

Born in Glasgow, Scotland, on 16 April 1890 but raised in Canada, Robert Leckie was at the controls of a Curtiss H-12 flying boat when he destroyed *L.22* on 14 May 1917 and served as rear gunner to Maj Egbert Cadbury on 5 August 1918 when they put paid to *L.70*, Frgkpt Peter Strasser and the entire Zeppelin offensive against Britain. He ultimately rose to the rank of air marshal in the Royal Canadian Air Force, dying in Ottawa on 31 March 1975. (Greg VanWyngarden)

On 5 August 1918, long after the *Luftstreitskräfte* gave up, Strasser led one more naval sortie against England. Only the demise of *L.70*, its crew and Strasser brought the Zeppelin bombing campaign to a suitably Wagnerian end.

Of a total of 115 airships produced during the war and employed on all fronts, 53 were destroyed and 24 too badly damaged to remain operational – an attrition rate of 40 per cent. Maj Robert Leckie, involved in the destruction of two of them, probably wrote the most succinct requiem:

The lesson of the airships is plain for all to read. The Germans had in their possession the most effective vehicle for fleet reconnaissance in any power's hands at that time. It was, at the same time, just about the world's worst strike aircraft!

British airmen credited with Zeppelin aerial victories

Pilot	Aeroplane	Unit	Airship	Date
Reginald A. J. Warneford	M-S L 3253	1 NAS	*LZ.37*	7/6/15
AAA/Claude A. Ridley and	BE 2c	No. 19 Res. Sqn	*L.15*	31/3/16
Albert de B. Brandon	BE 2c	No. 19 Res. Sqn		
William Leefe Robinson	BE 2c 2693	No. 39 (HD) Sqn	*SL.11*	3/9/16
AAA/A. de B. Brandon	BE 2c 4544	No. 39 (HD) Sqn	*L.33*	24/9/16
Frederick Sowrey	BE 2c 4112	No. 39 (HD) Sqn	*L.32*	24/9/16
Wulstan J. Tempest	BE 2c 4577	No. 39 (HD) Sqn	*L.31*	2/10/16
Ian V. Pyott	BE 2c 2738	No. 36 (HD) Sqn	*L.34*	27/11/16
Egbert Cadbury and	BE 2c 8625	Great Yarmouth	*L.21*	28/11/16
Gerard W. R. Fane and	BE 2c 8421	Great Yarmouth		
Edward L. Pulling	BE 2c 8626	Great Yarmouth		
Robert Leckie/John Galpin	H-12 8666	Great Yarmouth	*L.22*	14/5/17
Basil D. Hobbs/R. F. L. Dickey	H-12 8677	Great Yarmouth	*L.43*	14/6/17
F. D. Holder/S. Ashby and	FE 2b B401	Orfordness	*L.48*	17/6/17
Loudon P. Watkins and	BE 12 6610	No. 37 (HD) Sqn		
R. H. M. S. Saundby	DH 2 A5058	Orfordness		
Bernard A. Smart	Pup N6430	HMS *Yarmouth*	*L.23*	21/8/17
Egbert Cadbury/Robert Leckie	DH 4 A8032	Nos. 221/228 Sqns	*L.70*	5/8/18
Stuart D. Culley	Camel N6812	*H5*/HMS *Redoubt*	*L.53*	11/8/18

Leading Zeppelin Commanders

Captain	Airship(s)	British Raids
Horst *Freiherr* Treusch von Buttlar-Brandenfels	*L.6, L.11, L.30, L.25, L.54* and *L.72*	19
Heinrich Mathy	*L.9, L.13, L.31*	15
Werner Peterson	*L.7, L.12, L.16, L.32*	15
Erich Linnarz	*LZ.38, LZ.83* (Russia), *LZ.97*	9*

*Although his raid tally fell below those of his leading naval colleagues, Hptm Erich Linnarz held the distinction of commanding the first *Deutsches Heer* airship over England (29–30 April 1915), the first airship to be caught in a searchlight (17–18 May 1915) and the first to attack London (31 May–1 June 1915). Despite being hunted by such formidable opponents as Redford H. Mulock, Arthur Harris and William Leefe Robinson, Linnarz survived the war.

AFTERMATH

Even amid the Zeppelin bombing campaign, Ferdinand von Zeppelin's business endeavours were extending beyond the airships with which his name is indelibly associated. Embracing heavier-than-air craft with equal enthusiasm, he founded or generated such aviation spin-off firms as *Flugzeugbau* Friedrichshafen, builder of successful floatplanes and bombers, Zeppelin-Werke Lindau, in which Claude Dornier explored the use of Duralumin in flying boat and landplane structures, and Zeppelin-Werke Staaken, whose R VI was the only German multi-engined giant aeroplane to see anything resembling mass production.

Even when he switched to aeroplanes, Zeppelin thought big. Zeppelin-Staaken R VIs such as these operating with *Riesenflugzeug-Abteilung* 501, based at Sint-Denijs-Westrem, near Ghent, took part in an eventual 110 bombing raids on Britain, losing only four aeroplanes to enemy action. (Greg VanWyngarden)

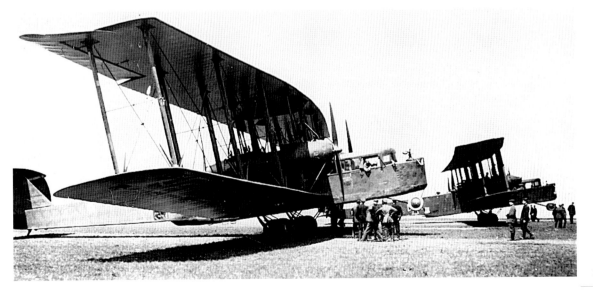

Airship development resumed in the realm of civil aviation after World War I. Arguably the most successful examples came from the builder with the most experience – *LZ.127 Graf Zeppelin*, seen here in Berlin in 1928, became the first aircraft to log more than a million miles of global transport. Its larger successor, *LZ.129 Hindenburg*, was destined for more notoriety than fame. (Courtesy of Airships.net)

By mid-1918 there were 15 Home Defence squadrons based in England with 166 fighters on strength, but by then their Bristol F 2Bs, Camels and SE 5as were defending primarily against aeroplanes, not airships. Besides Gotha bombers, their opponents were often Zeppelin-Staaken R-planes.

Ferdinand von Zeppelin died on 8 March 1917, but the foundations he laid endured Germany's defeat and the harsh terms of the Treaty of Versailles to resurrect the hydrogen-supported rigid airship in its original role, as a means of commercial air transport. Entering service in 1928, *LZ.127*, christened *Graf Zeppelin* in the late count's honour, entered service as the only aircraft to offer passage across the Atlantic Ocean, and when retired in 1937 it had made 590 flights totalling more than one million miles. The Zeppelin's revival was brought to an abrupt end by the fiery demise of *LZ.129 Hindenburg* at Lakehurst, New Jersey, on 6 May 1937 (along with its captain, Ernst A. Lehmann, who succumbed to his injuries the next day).

To a generation whose century of distance from the Zeppelin's heyday gives it the benefit of hindsight, the threat of these quaint oversized gasbags may be easier to dismiss now than at the time. It is another of those undeniable ironies of history, however, that the need to stop the lighter-than-air bombers spurred advances in heavier-than-air warplanes whose legacy endures today. Among those developments were pre-emptive strikes and interdiction, aerial night interception and shipboard operations using carrier-borne aircraft.

Much of what was learned in the course of eliminating the airship menace was readily applied to smaller, faster and more nimble targets when the Gothas and R-planes began to appear over British skies. For that matter, only radar constituted a significant game-changer to those formulae already established in World War I when the air campaign against Britain's homeland raged anew in the next war.

FURTHER READING

Brown, Richard, 'The day German bombers killed a hen in Maldon' (*Essex Chronicle*, 26 April 2015)

Belafi, Michael, *The Zeppelin* (Pen & Sword, 2015)

Bruce, J. M., *War Planes of the First World War: Volume Two* (Doubleday and Company, Inc., 1968)

Castle, Ian, *Osprey Campaign 193 – London 1914–17 – The Zeppelin Menace* (Osprey Publishing, 2008)

Cooksley, Peter, *BE 2 in Action* (Squadron/Signal Publications Inc., 1992)

Rimell, Raymond Laurence, *Zeppelin!* (Conway Martime Press Ltd, 1984)

INDEX

References to images are in **bold**.